JUNGLE PILOT
IN LIBERIA

JUNGLE PILOT
IN LIBERIA

ABE GUENTER

REGULAR BAPTIST PRESS
1300 North Meacham Road
Schaumburg, Illinois 60173-4888

Dedication

Without my dear wife, Susan, by my side these fifty-two years, the stories in this book could never have been realized. She also helped so much in the wording, corrections and proofreadings.

My daughter Suzanne did such a great job of rearranging, rewording, putting the whole book into the computer and running it off into the original manuscript.

Thanks to them, the whole family and our many friends for their encouragement and support. I dedicate this book to all of them.

Cover Photo Credit: Moody Bible Institute—Department of Missionary Aviation

Library of Congress Cataloging-in-Publication Data
Guenter, Abe, 1917–
    Jungle pilot in Liberia/Abe Guenter.
    p.   cm.
    ISBN 0-87227-169-2
    1. Missions—Liberia. 2. Aeronautics in missionary work—Liberia. 3. Guenter, Abe, 1917–   .   I. Title.
BV3625.L5G84   1992
266' .61' 092—dc20
[B]   92-6009
                                                                CIP

JUNGLE PILOT IN LIBERIA
©1992
Regular Baptist Press
Schaumburg, Illinois

Printed in U.S.A.
All rights reserved.

Second printing—1992

Contents

Foreword

The bush pilot is a fascinating individual with his skills, courage and ingenuity. But when that pilot is a missionary called of God to reach African people living in the rain forest jungles of Liberia, a story will unfold that will doubly capture your imagination and challenge your thinking.

Abe Guenter and his lovely wife, Susie, began their productive, innovative careers nearly fifty years ago and have invested a lifetime in missionary service. As a pioneer in missionary aviation, Abe early demonstrated the effectiveness of the airplane in reaching remote villages with the message of the gospel. His personal concern for the people and his willingness to help in times of need caused his name to be known throughout the country. As a result of his contacts and witness, many turned to Christ.

The development of the Baptist Mid-Missions radio network kept the pilot informed of existing needs and enabled him to respond to the requests of the mission family. Mail, supplies, medical evacuations, evangelistic trips and important personal contact with words of encouragement for isolated coworkers are all part of the day's work.

In this book the author relates stories of his many and varied experiences and provides an insightful look into life on the mission field. The reader will gain an understanding of the country, its customs and culture—but most importantly its people. Simple in style, graphic in description and Scriptural in content, this book reaches out to people of all ages. These stories will evoke a variety of emotions, but one is always left with a renewed sense of the faithfulness of the One Who said, "Lo, I am with you alway, even unto the end of the age."

For those who have not met Abe and Susie Guenter, this volume will serve as an introduction to two of God's choice servants. I am honored to have known them both as colaborers and friends.

Allan E. Lewis, President Emeritus
Baptist Mid-Missions

Pilot's Psalm*

The Lord is my Shepherd; the One Who guides me around clouds and mountains.

The Lord is my stability and strength, Who delivers me from fear.

The Lord is my Controller; I have two-way contact with Him every moment.

I shall not want for wisdom in difficult places, for He has promised me His wisdom.

He makes me to land safely in green valleys even though they are sometimes very small.

He leads me beside still rivers that point the way home.

He restores my calmness when flight has been frantic and quiets my heartbeat.

He walks on cloud as well as water and holds my plane in His hands through threatening storms.

Yes, even when I fly through dark, clouded valleys where I am in danger, I won't be afraid of Your purposes for me, for You are with me.

The ship didn't sink when You were sleeping in it;

Neither will my plane fall, for You are my Co-pilot—no, forgive me, Lord—rather I am Yours, and may I not forget it.

You bring me safely to places of unexpected fellowship and refreshment.

How good it is to be met at an airstrip by one of Your servants bringing a cool drink!

My cup is surely overflowing, for You have allotted the right number of days to my life, and You fill each day with good things to do for You. . . . Children to raise, planes to repair, interesting people to fly to important places on Your business—and so much more!

These things are goodness and mercy in tangible form.

And I will praise You for them through a safe and sure Eternity where we will roam a universe of sky and talk and love, You and I, forever and forever.

—The Informant

NOTE: Efforts to find the source of publication for this poem—and the poems on pages 22, 23, 62 and 93—were unsuccessful. The publisher would appreciate any information concerning the sources and would be pleased to include the sources in any subsequent editions of the book.

Oh Lord! (The Bull Story)

The week of studies had finished for the Bible school men. The "preacher boys" were eager to get going, so I began to fly them out, four at a time, to the many preaching centers. Each brought along his Bible and lantern as they loaded into the Super Cub.

When I dropped off the last load, two new Christian fellows asked to go with me to a far-off, deep jungle village in elephant country. So we took off. Ten miles from the village, I started pumping my throttle slowly, which gave a loud roaring signal that "Gantah" was going to spend the weekend with the villagers. It also meant for them to get on the airstrip and chase all the animals into the village to prepare for a safe landing. As I crossed over the end of the landing strip, I saw that the last animal was being chased off, so I lined up for a landing and prayed, "Thank You, Lord, for a safe flight over this beautiful yet treacherous jungle. Now, Lord, You know how many things can go wrong on a landing, so please watch over us again."

I throttled back, pulled back on the stick, pulled the flaps on and flared out for the uphill landing.

Just as I touched down, I saw him—a black bull—coming out of the jungle, trotting across the landing strip and heading for the village. The children had tried to chase him into the village too; but when he put his ugly horns down to charge them, they let him go, and he ran into the jungle. When he heard the airplane passing right over him, he got scared. He had but one place of safety, and that was the village across the airstrip. On he came, running right in front of me. We were on a collision course; what should I do?

I prayed my short emergency prayer: "Oh Lord!" and then I felt an inner urge to open the throttle wide. When that engine came to life with a roar, the bull changed his course and began trying to outrun me, but he didn't have a chance. I came up from behind him, and my right tire knocked his back legs out from under him, causing him to sit down on the struts. With his front legs still going, I pushed him for

40 feet. Then his front legs folded up under him, his nose went down, and I rolled right over him.

The right wing went way up, and when it came down, the plane went into a ground loop heading for the jungle. Two tall termite hills stood in my path, but the Lord graciously allowed me to go between them, or I might have been killed. Some stumps caught my landing gear, which slowed me down, and I got stopped with my propeller clipping through some soft branches of the thick jungle. The two men in the backseat screamed with fright, so I let them out first; and then I, too, hopped out.

First, I looked under the plane, and, sure enough, I still had wheels. But the damaged struts could no longer hold the wing. It came down slowly and rested on a tall stump. Those dear villagers felt so bad! Solemnly they came with their machetes to clear things away. Two men helped me push the wing up while I straightened the damaged struts somewhat. Then I asked for two six-foot poles and some of those strong vines hanging down from the tall jungle trees. With them, we reinforced my bent struts. Finally, as we were pulling the airplane back onto the landing strip, we heard the bull groaning. With a grunt for each leg, he managed to get back on all fours. Slowly he limped into the village. We hadn't even killed him!

I called Susie on the radio.

"Abe, you are excited!" she exclaimed.

"Yes," I replied. "I just ran into a bull with the airplane. I will have to spend the night here, preach and take time to check everything carefully, then try to fly home tomorrow." She had visions of a whole lot of beefsteak flying in with me, but the beefsteak was still walking!

I tied down the plane for the night, and as I pulled out my battery and small projector, the children began to dance. They ran into the village shouting out the good news.

"We will have pictures tonight—o!"

I asked for a table and looked for a whitewashed wall of a hut to use as a screen. As the sun dropped out of sight, the night turned suddenly dark. As the first picture appeared on the wall, the whole village came with their stools, benches and grass mats. They stayed with me as long as a picture gleamed on the wall. Bible pictures helped them greatly in understanding the Word.

The next morning, after singing, studying the Bible and praying, I prepared to leave. One of the believers came up to me, "Teachah

Gantah, you think the airplane can fly?"

"Yes, I think so, but you pray for me," I requested. I climbed in, kicked the starter and taxied up the hill. I swung the tail around with the power of the prop, checked my instruments and, with my usual prayer, I was ready for takeoff. With full power I raced down the hill and soon was airborne. Immediately I checked the plane for balance. It flew nicely, even though it looked kind of crude with the poles on the struts. I dipped my wing, made an about-face and headed home, praising the Lord for His protection, blessing and goodness.

Abe Guenter's Beginnings

W orld War I was just coming to an end when, on May 9, 1917, in a farmhouse 25 miles north of Saskatoon, Saskatchewan, Canada, a baby boy was born to Franz and Susanna Guenter. They were Mennonites, living among many others of the same heritage. They decided to call this third child Abraham, for it was a Mennonite custom to choose Bible names for their children.

As little Abe grew up, he became strong. He had a fighting spirit and liked to show off his great strength. Consequently he got into much trouble, and he lost his friends. Friendless and lonely, the boy began to search for something real, something to satisfy that deep longing in the heart that God has put into every human soul and that only God can satisfy.

The Guenters had a large farm, and Abe loved the animals. Father Franz bought Abe a wild horse from Alberta, fawn-colored with a black mane, black stripe along its back and a black tail. Taming that horse was a big job, but Abe finally did it, and the horse became his best friend. In winter Abe would tie a rope onto its tail and, with the horse pulling him, would have a lot of fun skiing up and down the snow drifts alongside the sleigh tracks.

Abe attended the local German school for three years. When the English school came to the village, he was eager to learn English. He loved school and did well. He also loved sports and was good at soccer, baseball and hockey. But still his heart had a void.

In the late fall of 1933, some evangelists preached in the schoolhouse. Young Abe, with his three brothers and two sisters, went every night and especially enjoyed all the new songs and choruses they were learning. Every night a Model T Ford came from the next village, loaded with happy young people. As they drove up to the school, they would sing

Jesus is real to me.
Yes, Jesus is real to me.
I never will doubt Him
Nor journey without Him,
For He is so real to me.

Inside during the meeting they would actually get up and testify that they were saved. This really touched young Abe's heart. Could you really know before you die that you are saved? How many times he had looked at that big stone pile on the end of the long field and said to himself, "I would gladly roll all those stones half a mile to the other end of the field if I could really know I was saved." Now he was hearing new and wonderful things:

"Believe on the Lord Jesus Christ, and thou shalt be saved. . . . He that believeth on him is not condemned. . . . He that believeth on the Son hath everlasting life. . . . But as many as received him, to them gave he power to become the sons of God, even to them that believe on his name" (Acts 16:31; John 3:18, 36; 1:12).

The evangelist declared, "Yes, you can be saved right now. Confess your sins, receive the Lord Jesus Christ as your own Savior, and He will never cast you out."

Someone has said, "You can lead a horse to water, but you can't make him drink." However, if you give the horse a handful of salt, he will go looking for water—and that is what was happening to Abe. Those young people were the salt of the earth, and they were feeding him salt. He came under deep conviction by the Holy Spirit and was thirsty for the Water of Life.

One night the evangelist preached on the return of the Lord, pointing out that He could come for believers any day. This really made Abe think. The Devil had been saying, "Yes, Abe, someday you should be saved but not just now. You have plenty of time; you are young and strong, and maybe you could not hold out anyway. It is hard being a Christian."

Then one night, as Abe sat with his buddies in the backseat, the evangelist appealed to people to go forward and pray. Conviction lay heavy on Abe, but he told himself, "I don't have to do it here in front of all these people and my buddies. I will go home and pray there." Upon arriving home, the family went inside the house, but Abe slipped behind the big barn and there knelt down by the tongue of the big wagon. "Oh God in Heaven, can you hear me? I am coming to You to confess my sins, and I now receive Jesus as my Savior. Please will You save my soul?" Then he looked up into Heaven, saw all the twinkling stars in the clear prairie sky and wondered if God had heard him. He decided to pray again and finally felt a little better in his heart, so he went to bed.

The next morning the Devil made a great mistake. "You are not saved; you're just kidding yourself," he told Abe. At this suggestion, Abe became desperate and, having lost all his pride, that night went forward to give himself publicly to Jesus. The preacher opened the Bible as they knelt beside a chair, carefully explained the way of salvation to him and asked him to pray, which he did.

"Did God hear you?" the preacher asked.

"Yes," Abe replied, "I believe He did." Then back into the Bible they went to John 6:37: "Him that cometh to me I will in no wise cast out."

"Tomorrow the Devil will come to you and say, 'You are not saved; you are kidding yourself,' but you tell him he is a liar. Just lean on God's promises every day and follow Jesus," the preacher continued. "Now, there is one more verse, Romans 10:10: 'For with the heart man believeth unto righteousness; and with the mouth confession is made unto salvation.' I want you to stand up now and tell these people what you have done." Abe shyly and nervously spoke up.

"Tonight I have received Jesus into my heart as my Savior, and I want to follow Him."

The meeting ended, and as Abe went out into the dark night, a great light shone into his heart. "For God, who commanded the light to shine out of darkness, hath shined in our hearts, to give the light of the knowledge of the glory of God in the face of Jesus Christ" (2 Cor. 4:6). That joy unspeakable and full of glory burst into his heart. Now it was impossible to contain all this glory and joy; he had to tell how wonderful Jesus is and that he really had been saved by the grace of God.

His uncle rebuked him declaring, "You must never say that you are saved—that is boasting. Say you *hope* to be saved. To *know* you are saved, you have to wait for the Judgment Day. Even the apostle Paul said, 'O wretched man that I am! who shall deliver me from the body of this death?' "(Rom. 7:24).

"But Uncle," Abe protested, "do you know the next verse?" He did not, but Abe did! " 'I thank God through Jesus Christ our Lord' " (Rom. 7:25). September 19, 1933, had been a great day, a second birthday for Abe.

The whole area began talking about him. What had really happened to Abe? He was so different; his bad ways and habits were gone, and he was always singing. "If any man be in Christ, he is a new creature: old things are passed away; behold, all things are become new" (2 Cor. 5:17). It was a miracle, and he just could not keep it in. He went to all the youth meetings and gave his testimony. He even handed out tracts, and young people were listening and reading.

Abe's family was unsaved; but one-by-one they, too, began to turn to Jesus. One winter day as Abe read his Bible in the big farmhouse kitchen and his mother sat close by the table doing some needlework, she watched him intently reading his Bible. "Abe, you should not read that Bible so much. Some people go crazy from reading it too much."

"Oh no, Mother, this is the joy and rejoicing of my heart; it is food for my soul. I get so blessed from reading it," he protested fervently.

"I wish I could also know that I am saved," his mother sighed, with a tear rolling down her cheek. Shortly after that, she also came to know the Lord; and now the whole family was saved except Dad. The others began to pray for him in earnest until one day he became deathly sick. Then he, too, called upon the name of the Lord. The whole family was now complete in the Lord Jesus.

Abe Learns to Pray

From the first day of his "new birth," Abe found joy in spending time with the Lord in prayer. He knew many unsaved people to pray for, and it was a joy to see the Lord answer his prayers.

He realized he needed a secret place of prayer and found just the place in the hayloft above the animals in the barn. At times his father would call for him, but he felt that when he talked to his Heavenly Father, he must not interrupt that sacred time with a response to his earthly father. So he just kept on praying until he was finished.

When it got too cold in the hayloft, he found a place in the attic of the house. One day he was deep in prayer on his knees with his head down on the floor when his oldest sister came up and found him there. She was scared when he did not move. She finally spoke. "Abe, what are you doing here?"

"Please, won't you just leave me alone when I pray?" he pleaded with tears in his eyes.

One night, riding home on his bike from prayer meeting, he remembered he had not yet finished praying for all the people on his list that day. He never actually wrote down a list. His list was names written in his heart, and it just kept growing until it took a half hour and sometimes a whole hour to pray through. What should he do? It was nearly midnight, but he stopped on top of a hill and knelt down beside the road to finish his praying for the day. The moon shone beautifully, and the stars twinkled brightly in the dark prairie sky; he lost all track of time as he bathed himself in the glory of God with tears gliding down his cheeks. Finally he climbed back onto his bike and pedalled home to the farm, well past midnight.

Daybreak came at 4:30 A.M., and not long afterward, Father called the boys to get up and prepare for the day's work on the farm. Abe woke up refreshed. "But they that wait upon the LORD shall renew their strength; they shall mount up with wings as eagles; they shall run, and not be weary; and they shall walk, and not faint" (Isa. 40:31).

Later, in Bible college, the studies would overwhelm Abe, and he had a hard time finding a secret place. Though it was against the rules to leave one's room after 10:00 P.M., he would steal out into the chapel to be alone with God. One night the principal discovered him there on his knees. He came over and put his hand on Abe's head. "What are you doing here, Abe?"

"I had to find a secret place for prayer," he responded, with tear-filled eyes.

Then Abe discovered that the hour before the wake-up bell in the morning, when everyone was still sleeping, was a good time for private prayer. He found that, though he lost an hour of sleep, he was wide awake in class while others at times could hardly keep their eyes open.

Abe, Sell That Bike!

I was sixteen and needed transportation to witness for Christ, so I began to collect second-hand parts for a bicycle. Finally I had all the parts, assembled them into a bike, painted it and loved it. It was my great helper to go witnessing and attend meetings. I especially loved prayer meetings, and, come rain, snow or shine, I would be there.

One night as I went home from prayer meeting, riding the five miles in the dark, I followed the light strips where the wheels of cars had smoothed the road. I was just barely able to see enough to keep going, for I had no light. All of a sudden the front wheel hit a big rock, and I went sprawling flat on the road. I picked myself up and found I was not badly hurt. The bicycle was not damaged either, so I continued on my way home, praising the Lord.

Around that time, a voice kept telling me, "Abe, sell that bicycle." This imperative continued for about a week, and finally I prayed before going to bed:

"Lord Jesus, tomorrow that bike will be sold unless You restore the peace to my heart." Next morning, God gave me back His perfect peace. Then I knew it had been a test of my love and obedience, something like that of the Biblical Abraham.

Abe the Missionary

I was determined to really serve the Lord and longed to go to Bible college. Going up and down the long fields while I farmed, I had time to sing, think and pray. At the end of the field I would rest my horses and sink my knees into the soft earth I had plowed. I had read in my Bible, "Pray ye therefore the Lord of the harvest, that he will send forth labourers into his harvest" (Matt. 9:38), so I began to pray, "Lord, would You send out missionaries? So many millions in faraway lands have never heard Your gospel. Please, Lord, send someone to tell them the good news."

As I continued to pray like that, I heard the voice of God speaking in my spirit: "I want *you* to go."

"Me?" I exclaimed. "I am just a boy on this farm. I can't do much— can't even give a good testimony; my tongue is so heavy, like Moses."

"But look what I did with Moses!" He replied.

"Then here am I, send me. If you can use me, I would be so delighted to be a missionary," I said with all my heart. That fall the Lord opened the way for me to attend the Saskatoon Bible College.

The next spring I joined the Canadian Sunday School Mission and went out on my bike with my guitar slung on the side. I drove a hundred miles northwest and began my first missionary outreach. I conducted VBS from school to school and even preached at night. It was hard pedalling that bike over hills and valleys, up to 75 miles some days, but as a good soldier of Christ I was learning to endure hardness. It was good training and body building for Africa. Hard days, yes, but happy days, for souls were coming to Jesus, and that made even the angels in Heaven rejoice.

Money was hard to come by to go back to Bible school, but the Lord made a way. There came a Sunday, however, when I was down to ten cents, which was enough for a ride on the streetcar from church back to the college to arrive in time for dinner. It was a long walk to the church, but with the dime in my pocket, I would at least have a ride back.

It was great being in church with God's wonderful people, but before the sermon, the deacons took up the offering. Now the plates were coming closer, back and forth along the long rows, and my dime was starting to burn a hole in my pocket. A still, small voice said, "Put in that dime," but I doubted what to do. I knew I would miss dinner if I walked back to the college. Then the plate was coming right down my row, and again that small voice said, "Put it in." Now the plate was in front of me. I quickly thrust my hand into my pocket and plunked in that dime. As soon as I had done it, a great joy flooded my soul.

The sermon was so good, and the people seemed loving and kind. Finally I found myself out on the street, walking back to school. I felt as though I were walking on air, and I was singing as I passed the streetcar that should have carried me back. Then a nice old lady inside shouted, "Abe, come in. I will pay your way." I ran over and sat down beside her.

"Thank you, thank you!" I exclaimed. Then she opened her purse, pulled out a whole dollar bill and gave it to me.

"This is for you too," she said graciously.

"Really?" I gasped in surprise.

"Yes," she said firmly. I thanked her profusely as I began to realize I had paid my tithe in advance with my dime. I have been a tither ever since (Mal. 3:10).

I Am a Missionary

If I am God's man in God's place, I am a missionary.
If doing God's work in God's grace, I am a missionary.

So, whether here or far away,
Let me the call of God obey;
If I am God's man in God's place, I am a missionary.

                                    —*Author Unknown*

A Wife for Abe

When Abe surrendered to the Lord for missionary service, He planned to be single, like the apostle Paul, but something else happened. One of those lovely young people who had come in the Model T to the meetings where he had been saved was now coming occasionally to the prayer meeting Abe attended so faithfully. She was beautiful, and she smiled so sweetly at him that he knew something sweet was happening in his heart. Yet he did not think this feeling was the will of God for him. He struggled with this sweet feeling and asked God to take it away. But instead of it going away, it grew stronger and stronger.

One night Abe desperately prayed, "Lord, if it is Your will for me to marry this wonderful girl, please reveal Your will to me, even if by a dream tonight." He had read in his Bible how God had answered in this way many times before, so he believed God could answer in this way for him too.

That night he had a dream. He dreamed he was climbing the stairs in a big building. When he was halfway up, he turned to continue up. Then he noticed that this Susie Kasper was just two steps ahead of him. When he took his first step, she took her third and then stopped and turned toward him. When Abe finished two more steps, she reached out her hand, and they continued together. He awoke and, of course, it was only a dream, but it fit! He had reached a definite turning point in his life. He was taking his first year of Bible school, and she was taking her third. Hence the first and third steps of the dream had some significance.

After his graduation, Abe went south to within a few miles of Montana, where he became a pastor. By that time he loved Susie so much that he could not continue being without her. Since he needed help for the VBS work, he went back to Saskatoon and married that beautiful girl. Then they labored together.

Susie also had had a call to Africa, and presently the Lord gave them both a great burden for Liberia. After three years of ministry in Saskatchewan, they went to British Columbia for some further training before leaving for Liberia. By this time the Lord had given them two wonderful sons, and people asked Abe, "Are you going to take your beautiful family to the 'white man's grave'?" He always answered, "Yes. The Lord has promised, '. . . Lo, I am with you always . . .' (Matt. 28:20). He will protect us."

The Heathen live not knowing why they were born,
And die not knowing why they have lived.

Is it not a sin that here so few have so much,
When over there so many have so little?

You cannot give to God and lose.
                                                    —*Source Unknown*

Departure for Pennsylvania

We left Chilliwack, British Columbia, in late May of 1945, with many farewells and tears. Mother and Dad shed tears but encouraged us and promised to pray for us. Our old Chevy took us safely to Saskatchewan, where we sold it. Kissing friends good-bye there, we boarded the train for Toronto to spend a little time with Gordon and Catherine Mellish, veteran missionaries to Liberia under Baptist Mid-Missions.

Catherine nearly died once in the early '40s when she had to be carried out by hammock, a five days' journey to medical help. Harlan Rahilly helped to bring her out and, having been a pilot for Le Tourneau, he said, "Oh, if only we had an airplane, how wonderful it would be!" That was the beginning of a vision for an aviation ministry in Liberia with Baptist Mid-Missions.

After much encouragement from the Mellishes, we again boarded the train for Lock Haven, Pennsylvania. We were met by Pastor Howard G. Young of First Baptist Church, the church that had adopted us as their missionaries. The next morning was the last Sunday of June, and we enjoyed the services and fellowship of those dear people so much.

On Monday the pastor said, "I want to introduce you to Mr. William Piper who builds the Piper Cub airplanes right here." We went to the factory and right into his office. The old gentleman squeezed my hand warmly.

"Abe, if you are going to Africa to be a missionary, you must take an airplane with you, but first you must learn to fly."

"Yes, sir!" I agreed. He kept talking, and I kept saying, "Yes, sir!"

Finally he said, "I tell you what we will do. We will train you free of charge."

"Yes, sirrrrr!" I responded immediately.

In a day or two I got my first lesson from Curt Wetzel, a member in the church and also his best test pilot. How I have thanked God for this man who had had the highest rating in Fort Worth, Texas, as an instructor during the war. He gave me a rough time with his thorough training technique though. He would shout at me during flight, "That was a lousy turn. I don't think you will ever learn to fly!" I was so discouraged until one day his wife told me,

"Abe, Curt tells me you are doing exceptionally well."

"Me?" I exclaimed. Then she began to laugh.

"That is his technique." I felt so much better after that!

After just seven hours of instruction one morning, I was surprised when Curt climbed out of the plane and announced, "It's all yours; take it around." I took off all alone and brought it down again nice and smoothly. Curt made me take it around two more times and then took me over to the testing area and told the boys, "Abe soloed."

The guys just stood there, so he prodded, "Aren't you going to do something?" They were not sure if they dared to do the usual to this preacher. With me sitting in the rear seat, one came from each side of the car, grabbed the back of my shirt and tore it into pieces. Then they took a piece to the office and hung it up with my name on it, announcing to all that I had become a pilot.

Forced Landing in a Pasture

Two days later as I was practice-flying and building up my experience and hours for my private license, the engine quit on me. I was doing my stalls at 2,000 feet, just ten miles west of the city. About the third time, as I pulled the stick way back, the engine slowed down and actually stopped turning, with the propeller stuck in an up-and-down position. "Oh Lord!" I prayed, and then, as I had been taught, I pushed the stick forward to regain flying speed.

Looking around for a place to set the plane down, I saw a long pasture right in front of me. I came down slowly with a dead stick. Some cows were in the pasture, but they cooperated nicely. I touched down, let her roll, then braked to a gentle stop. Two very surprised boys came from the nearby fishing creek with their poles in hand, looked me over and kindly agreed to hold the plane while I hand-cranked it. With a cough and a splutter, it came to life. I thanked them, jumped in, swung the plane around and took off.

After landing at the airport, I called Curt. "Curt, I had a forced landing."

"Where are you?" he demanded.

"At the operations tower," I replied. He jumped into one of the Cubs he had tested and flew over. He was extremely upset.

"Where is the plane?"

"Right there," I said, pointing to it. Then he began to chew me out.

"Didn't you know you weren't supposed to fly out a downed aircraft? Nobody except a licensed mechanic can do that!"

"How was I supposed to know?" I replied. "You never told me." He tried to act angry, but his pride in his pupil showed through too much!

After 50 hours of flying time, I qualified for my private ticket, and then Mr. Piper asked me to serve as a ferry pilot. The war had come to an end, and now yellow paint was being sprayed over the army green on the Cubs to prepare them for the many dealers who were crying, "Send us Piper Cubs!" I had fun and great experiences flying the new Cubs over country I had never seen. I had no radio—just a compass and my map. What wonderful training for the primitive conditions on the mission field, and I was being paid for it too!

Departure for Liberia (Liberia at Last?)

Finally, after nine wonderful months at Lock Haven—flying, preaching, buying and packing equipment—we were ready. Then word came from the travel agent in New York that they had found seats for us in a converted C54 Pan Am passenger plane. We were excited! What a day that was when we finally took off for Africa, together with Nadyne Ricks, a fellow missionary under Baptist Mid-Missions. From New York, we touched down in Newfoundland, Iceland, Ireland, Portugal (for the night) and Dakar. After 36 hours of flying, we finally landed at Roberts Airport in Liberia. We will never forget how, when the doors were opened at 2:00 A.M. March 22, 1946, that steamy tropical air rushed into the plane, and we knew we had arrived. It almost felt like an oven door had been opened. Our hosts guided us to the Army barracks, where we tried to get a few hours of sleep on some army cots.

At daybreak, we meandered over to the U.S. Army mess hall for breakfast and then tried to find a way into the city of Monrovia, which was 55 miles away. The missionaries in Monrovia had no telephone or radio, so we could not tell them that we had arrived. Finally we, together with some other missionaries, were able to hire a truck with a little house built on the back for passengers. It was slow going. As darkness fell, we came to a chugging stop. The driver and others tore off the hood, pushed and shoved, but the old truck had really died. When they opened the distributor and broke the rotor, I knew we were in trouble. But just before dark, a U.S. Army jeep pulled alongside and kindly took the women and children into the city, while we men stayed with the baggage. As we waited for help, we decided it would be smart to roll down our sleeves to protect us from the malaria-carrying mosquitoes. In the darkness we saw some headlights coming, and the vehicle stopped. The passengers were U.S. Navy men, and they kindly rescued us too. That night, when our sons bedded down under the mosquito net, I saw great beads of perspiration on their bare backs, but they slept. Finally the rest of us got to bed and slept some.

The next morning Nadyne Ricks almost turned around to go home, for the food, the heat and the smell of the pigs living under the guest house were just too much for her. We were able to encourage her, however, and she went into the interior with us a few days later.

We hired one of the two city trucks to take us the 120 miles to

Suakoko station. The road was not too bad for a while. But then it became narrower and narrower, and finally there were no more bridges—just planks for the wheels. I really began to pray. "Lord, help the driver not to miss the planks," for I rode on top of our load looking ahead and could see everything. We climbed a hill, and when we came down the other side, the driver actually speeded up to cross the planks and labor up the next hill. I got so scared! We traveled all day; then just as the sun dipped behind the hills and the daylight vanished, we arrived and were warmly welcomed by the missionaries.

Suakoko station was a mile from the village of Suakoko, named after a woman chief who had died. What interesting people! The villagers were mostly naked worshipers of idols, hills, rivers, ancestors and spirits.

They made their houses entirely of jungle materials. First, they drove poles into the ground in a circle, tied them together with vines and plastered them with mud. They fashioned the roof with poles and thatch, and tied it together with vines. They found white chalk in the ground, which they used to whitewash the walls. The cottonwood trees had wide, flat roots above ground, which the people chopped off and made into doors. They leveled the floors and smeared them with mud by hand. Their beds were raised places along the wall onto which they rolled their grass mats. The smoke from the fire in the middle of the floor would drive out the mosquitoes. It was too hot and smoky for us, but not for the nationals. The people were friendly and gave us their best woven chairs. However, before long, we could feel the bites of the bedbugs on our seats—ouch!

The Stabbed Man

One night we heard the beating of native drums in town. They grew louder and louder. Though we lived a mile away, the noise was so intense that we could not sleep. Then suddenly a great cry went up with screaming and shouting, and before long we heard the people coming our way. We wondered, "What now?" Soon lanterns and torches appeared on the mission station, and everybody talked at the same time. Then we saw a hammock—with someone in it—being carried by four men. They showed us a dagger covered with blood, which had been stuck into the back of the man in the hammock. We quieted down the crowd, fixed a bed in the clinic for the man and dressed his wound. We prayed with him and told him about Jesus.

After midnight we left him in the hands of one of the few believers and went to bed. Up again at 5:30, we wondered about and prayed for our sick man.

When we opened the clinic door, we noticed he was awake and apparently quite alert. Then a great crowd came from the village. They had the man they called the killer: naked, a chain around his waist and a big cross tied to his back. They continually beat him and insisted that they had to carry our sick man along to the district commissioner to make a full investigation. It was a ten-mile walk (we had no transportation in those days); we knew such a journey would kill the stabbed man, so we refused. Finally the crowd left, and we continued to minister to our patient.

Again we talked to him about Jesus, the Way, the Truth and the Life. He opened his heart to the Lord, and a wonderful change came over him. We rejoiced and prayed that he would get well and perhaps become our first evangelist among his people. He kept on improving, even walking; but this incident took place before the days of penicillin, and infection set in. Within a week he faded away from this life, but his last words were, "Jesus! Oh, Jesus!" One day we will see him coming down the streets of Glory, and we will rejoice again. "I am not ashamed of the gospel of Christ: for it is the power of God unto salvation to every one that believeth . . ." (Rom. 1:16).

My First Jungle Trek

I had been asked to preach through an interpreter in the little church on the mission. It was hard, and I felt lost in this jungle country where everything was new. I had so much to learn.

One day I took three schoolboys with me as I went to preach in the villages. I carried my rifle, chop (food) box, lantern, camp cot and mosquito net. The boys talked so loudly I decided that if I were going to find some game, I would have to go ahead a bit.

Soon I lost sight of them, and then I heard them shouting and screaming. It sounded as if they were really in trouble. I raced back and found them up in the trees. "What are you boys doing up there?" I demanded.

"Teacher, a bush cow came and chased us," they said, shaken. I saw one of the boys in a thorn tree that had thorns two inches long.

"But how did you get up there?" I wondered. He looked rather bewildered.

"I don't know."

"Come on down; let's get out of here," I said, and he jumped straight down about seven feet. He must have jumped straight up there in one leap in his deathly fright. I learned that the villagers considered the bush cow to be the meanest wild animal.

We pressed on and arrived at the village late in the afternoon. The people welcomed us and gave us a hut to sleep in, so we set up my cot and net for the night. After supper and a preaching service, I rolled onto my cot, and the boys slept around me on the floor.

In the middle of the night I heard screaming, crying and wailing. I became extremely scared! I thought the mob was coming to get me. I woke one of the boys and whispered, "Peter, what is going on? Tell me!"

"Teacher," he explained, "someone has died just now, and they are crying the death wail." I relaxed but cried inside. Had we come too late?

We stayed over Sunday and had several services with the whole village. The chief spoke for all the people. "We all believe on Jesus now." The gospel was so new to them, and the villagers always looked to their chief to lead them. So I wondered, "Is it real?"

The Cub Arrives

When June came, we got the word that our Piper J3 Cub had arrived, so Harlan Rahilly and I took a money-bus (a truck for passengers) to Monrovia. When I saw only one crate for the airplane, my spirits plummeted. "Harlan, they forgot to send the wings. How are we going to fly it without wings?"

"Don't get excited, Abe," he said calmly. "Let's look inside." When we tore a board loose from the top, we peeked inside and found the wings neatly stashed alongside the fuselage, attached to the walls of the crate.

In no time we had the crate apart and the airplane together. We test-flew the Cub on July 4, 1946. Now we had wings for Liberia. Harlan flew the plane first. When he came down, he said, "Abe, the compass is stuck."

"Let me try it," I suggested. I took the plane up and decided to loop it a few times. When I did, the compass began to work again, so then everything tested out. Since Harlan had more experience, we decided that he should fly the plane up-country.

I raced on ahead by truck to prepare for the momentous landing on our 900-foot airstrip. It was a great day! Everybody turned out, including the chief, and did he strut around!! After all, wasn't he the only chief in Liberia with an airplane at his village?

A Conference and New Mission Airstrips

So many of us new missionaries had arrived in so short a time after the war that we needed to come together to decide where each of us would serve. A truckload of us left Suakoko for the end of the road 13 miles farther on. From there we trekked by jungle trails for five more hours to the Yila station on the Saint John River. Our two boys had a hammock to ride in, carried on the heads of natives, while the rest of us strode along the trail. That was fun for a while. But in the heat of the day our shoes began to chafe our heels, and stones and stumps caused us to stumble and sometimes fall. A big soldier ant managed to get to my toe and actually snip off a piece of flesh when I pulled him off, so we learned to respect and jump over that kind of ant. When we came to a log over a creek, we found a whole army of those ants crossing it already. We rolled up our pants and took a run over the log and the ants, then quickly brushed them off before they could start their vicious attack.

When we arrived, the missionaries from Yila and Tappi stations welcomed us. We had a wonderful time in prayer, in the Word and in planning our future ministries. The other missionaries asked us to go to the Bassa tribe, deep in the jungles of Liberia.

Soon after the conference, Harlan was able to fly into Yila for the first time, and a month later on one of my flights to Yila, Dick Miller told me he had received word that the Tappi airfield was also finished.

There was no map of Liberia with which to plan the flight. "Dick," I said, "let's go. You show me the way, and maybe we can find it." With a high ceiling, we were able to climb way up into the sky, and after 15 minutes' flight I looked to my left and saw an unusually large village in the distance. "Dick, is that Tappi?" I yelled over the engine noise.

"Maybe," he responded, so I banked to my left. Soon we flew over the station and saw the new long landing strip.

As we circled a bit, we saw the village empty out, all running to see the iron bird come down. What excitement! Even the old chief came running, wanting to see the man in that iron bird and maybe shake his hand and snap his finger the way all Liberians do. We had found Tappi.

Later Gordon Mellish whispered to me, "Abe, that old chief is the paramount chief for this whole area, and he is still a cannibal." I was learning many things and hoped he would not eat me! The Mellishes, who had pioneered this station, were happy to have air service too. The vision of an aviation ministry had resulted from Catherine's earlier brush with death.

Lepers, Get Out!

The Nickersons, fellow missionaries, had approached the government about starting a leprosy colony at Suakoko. The officials were pleased with the idea but jumped the gun on them, for we had not had time to plan and prepare for these hopeless souls.

The officials sent soldiers into the villages in the area to drive all the lepers out, forcing them to go to the mission. Were we shocked! About 230 lepers came hobbling onto the compound in one day. What were we going to do with them? Art Nickerson, the head of the station, talked kindly to the great crowd and asked them to go to the other side of the road that passed through the mission and there construct shelters for themselves.

This plan amazed me! The lepers went into the forest and came back with poles, vines and thatch. Some of the lepers had no fingers or toes and were in sad condition, but others helped to build shelters for them too. Before nightfall, a new village stood on the other side of the road.

I asked Art if I might go to the new village morning and evening to minister to the lepers, and he gladly consented. So I took my guitar, and a native man and I began teaching them songs, Bible verses and stories, always making the gospel as simple and clear as we could. We had to meet out in the open space between the huts. God began to bless, and souls were saved.

One man, Flumo, came every day, morning and evening, but he had to crawl on all fours. Always he sat in the same place, leaning against a palm tree. One day the Holy Spirit opened his heart, and he, too, was gloriously saved. After that day he came with a great smile on his thin, wrinkled face, for he knew he was going to Heaven.

One morning I noticed that no one sat by the palm tree. After the meeting I asked, "Where is Flumo?" The other lepers said they had not seen him that day, so we walked over to his hut and in Liberian fashion called, "Bock, bock, bock." There was no answer. I pushed open the crude bamboo door, and there he lay, all curled up on his grass mat, just skin and bones. But no, he really was not there; the angels had carried him to Glory.

The others looked in and said, "Aye yah. Flumo is dead. We must bury him. Please give us a shovel, and we will dig a hole and then call you."

In the early afternoon they called me for the burial service. They had dug a hole and tied his body in his grass mat. Then they tied his hands together and his feet together, inserting a long pole between his hands and feet. Two men, a man on each end, grabbed the pole and swung it onto their heads, leaving Flumo's body dangling down between them as they carried him to the small, shallow grave. When they laid him down, they placed the pole on the ends of the grave, leaving the body hanging inside the grave.

"We are ready," they announced. "Please bring us the words of God now." I was shocked. What a sight! How could I preach? What should I say? Then 1 John 3:2 came to me clearly: "Beloved, now are we the sons of God. . . ." I was overwhelmed with the grace of God to this poor miserable wretch, now transported from his skin-and-bone corpse into the very presence and glory of Christ. After the message and an appeal for others to believe on Jesus, I closed in prayer and told them to bury him.

But I had another shock coming. The men on each end of the grave lowered their machetes in unison, chopping the ropes that tied Flumo's hands and feet. Then Flumo's body dropped down into the grave with a thud. The others joined in, pushing the dirt on top of him with their hands and with the shovel. I could not get over what I had seen. The passage I had spoken from continued to glow in my heart: ". . . and it doth not yet appear what we shall be: but we know that, when he shall appear, we shall be like him; for we shall see him as he is" (1 John 3:2). What a gospel to preach to all the world!

Mary, I Am Not Dead!

Word had come through the jungles that Bob Smith, who ministered in the middle of the Bassa tribe, was deathly sick and might already have died. I gassed up the airplane and prepared to fly out to see. Again I had no map, and again the terrain was all dense jungle with nothing to guide me. I prepared three identical letters to drop. The letters read, "Hi! If Bob Smith is better, spread one bed sheet on the ground. If Bob Smith is worse, spread two bed sheets on the ground. If Bob Smith is dead, spread three bed sheets on the ground."

I hand-cranked the engine. Then sitting in the cockpit, I prayed, "Lord, You know that I don't know the way, but would You please guide me to that needle-in-the-haystack Zondo station and keep me safe over that beautiful jungle?" It was a 30-minute flight and, sure enough, I found the station. Bob had built a rather large, long, mud-stick, thatch-roofed house right on the top of a hill. When I circled, I saw Mary, his wife, come out.

I crumpled up the three letters and, flying low in front of their house, I threw the letters out the window. They fluffed open and fluttered down right in front of the house. Mary grabbed one, read it hastily and ran into the house. Then Bob appeared, extremely thin, feeble and unsteady on his feet. He, too, grabbed a letter and read. Mary started to spread out three bed sheets on the ground. When Bob saw that, he hollered, "Mary! What are you doing? I'm not dead! Pick up two of those sheets."

I was up there circling and chuckling to myself! I could see Bob was getting better. I throttled back and yelled down, "Hi, Bob! It's so good to see you on your feet again. I will walk in to help you build that airstrip." Then I flew back, rejoicing and bearing the good news to all the rest.

A Big Trek and a Big Scare

The time had come for me to make that six-day walking trip into the Bassa tribe to build the airfield so we could join Bob and Mary Smith and Virginia Lillard in winning that tribe for Jesus. The chief gave me seven men to carry my loads and Henry, a Christian Bassa man, to guide and interpret. The rainy season was upon us, and all the rivers were flooded. But we made good progress, stopping here and there to preach and to sleep in the native huts along the way.

We came to a creek that had swollen into a rushing river. The bridge of logs lay deep under the water, and when I stood on it, hanging onto a pole that had been tied to the trees, the water reached up to my neck.

"You think you can make it?" I asked Flumo, one of the carriers.

"Yes, I can," he replied. Then he took off all his clothes, tied them on top of my suitcase, took a deep breath and completely disappeared under the water until he emerged on the other side. Fortunately, my things in the suitcase stayed dry. He put his few clothes back on, and we continued on our way.

We approached a large village. At the entrance many hornbill birds sat in tall trees. My men asked me to bring one down for dinner, so I took careful aim and shot one through his big bill. He came flapping down. Just fluid—no blood—ran from his bill. My bullet had pierced his bill and destroyed his equilibrium so he couldn't even stand up. As my men wrung his neck, the villagers came, shouting, "Please don't shoot our gods! Our grandparents are living in those birds; they are our gods."

"No, they are not gods," I countered. "Come, let me tell you about the real God." So we had another opportunity to preach the gospel of the living God. The people listened well.

"Why have you not told us this Good News before?" they demanded. "Can't you stay awhile and tell us more?" With heavy hearts we moved on and on and on.

Another day, when all our meat was gone, the men begged, "Teacher, can you please shoot that black bird on that far-away tree for our dinner?" I looked down that long straight trail and saw him. I steadied my rifle against a small tree and, aiming high to allow for the bullet to drop and with a prayer on my lips, I pulled the trigger and saw the bird fall straight down. The men ran ahead and picked it up. Were they happy! "Thank You, Lord."

We had walked till mid-afternoon and came to a village. The people were glad to see us and asked us to stay for the night. "No," I declined. "The way is too long, and we must move on."

"No teacher," they protested. "The river is too high."

"Well, will you let us preach to you if we stay?" I asked.

"Yes, that is what we want," they responded gladly. They were hungry to hear the Word of God! In the morning they begged us to stay, but after another time of preaching we had to move on. We walked and walked. Finally I paused.

"Henry, where is that river?" He looked embarrassed.

"Teacher, there is no river here."

"You mean those people lied to us about the flooded river?" I asked, surprised.

"Yes, teacher," he answered. "They were hungry to hear the Word of God."

"Then we can forgive them, Henry," I decided. God impressed upon me anew that a whole world is out there hungry for something, they know not what. Until they are satisfied with the Bread of Life, they will remain hungry. Why don't we have more missionaries? Christ's last command should be our first concern. ". . . Go ye into all the world, and preach the gospel . . ." (Mark 16:15).

On the fifth day, toward evening, I was tired of the jungle and longed for a bit of civilization. According to the schedule someone had given me, the Gay Peter mission station was only 30 minutes further and, though the sun was about to set, I felt I could make it.

"The road is far a little bit," Henry commented.

"I can make it," I declared. "Who will go with me?" One man in the village volunteered, so we left. All I had was a flashlight, and when the sun dropped down, the way was extremely dark, but we stumbled on. We came to a river, where the bridge was just a big log and the water rushed over it. Carefully and slowly, with the aid of my dim flashlight, we made it. Then we pushed on.

By then we had trekked through the jungle an hour, and I began to wonder what was happening. I had heard about the Bassa Devil Bush and wondered if this stranger was leading me to it. I kept following on and on, however, until finally I saw a light at the end of a long straight path, flanked on either side by carefully planted palm trees. My guide pointed ahead excitedly, and I knew we had arrived. It had been one and a half hours instead of half an hour.

Gay Peter was staffed by two single ladies, Emma Wisser and Kay Tullis. They welcomed me warmly and fixed me a delicious dinner and warm bath. It was good to be in a comfortable home! Then I noticed a lot of excitement among the native girls, so I asked, "What's going on?"

"Oh," Miss Wisser answered, "the girls asked me some time ago when I was going to get married. I told them, 'Never, unless God drops a man from Heaven.' Now, they have heard that you fly in the sky and have dropped down in the night, and they are saying, 'This is it. We are going to have a wedding!' " The girls were disappointed to learn I was already married.

By Monday morning my carriers and Henry had caught up with me, and we made the final one-day push to Zondo to be with Bob and Mary Smith and to help them with the airfield. After receiving a royal welcome, I stayed about a week overseeing the building of the airstrip but doing no physical labor. My heart had been pumping hard all the way on the long trek and wanted to continue its fast-paced pumping. I noticed my whole camp bed actually moved back and forth with the heavy action of my heart. It scared Bob (and me too), so he rounded up four men to carry me in a hammock 40 miles down to the coast. I got in the hammock and rode in it about half a mile. But I did not like it, so I got out and started to walk. The more I walked, the better I felt; so I sent the carriers back and made the two-day walk just fine. At Buchanan City, I told my story to a doctor.

"Your heart just wanted to keep going," he said. "You are in good shape." I was happy to accept his diagnosis. Then I traveled in a small boat to Monrovia and finally home to Suakoko on a money-bus. It was good to see my family again! We were excited now about moving down to Zondo.

Christmas in a Native Hut

A week before Christmas, Susie, the boys (Wesley and Darrell) and I flew down to Zondo, about 75 air miles. We moved right into the middle of a native village and into a native hut, which was full of big long rats and many other creeping things—possibly even snakes— that lived in the thick thatch roof. Living in the hut and village was a new way of life for us. The native children and adults gawked at us through our windows day and night. When I put up some screens, they pushed, poked and shoved until the screens came off and they could again watch these funny white people with their strange ways. But God gave us His love to love these black, nearly naked, heathen people. Soon they began to love us too, and we had the joy of winning them for our God.

Christmas came, and we tried to generate a little Christmas spirit by building a Christmas tree with branches of a tree that resembled a real pine tree. I drilled some holes into a pole, stuck branches into it—and the artificial Christmas tree was born! We had brought some tree ornaments, and Susie and the boys made some. It wasn't a *white* Christmas, but it was a *good* Christmas.

Where Is the Monkey?

Living in the native hut in Zondo town was an experience we will never forget. We did not see the rats in the thatch during the day, but at night they took over and went everywhere, even in our dresser drawers. They ran back and forth along the head of our bed, then up the net and back into the thatch. I assume they were looking for food, or maybe they were just visiting or trying to scare us! We had mosquito nets that kept them away from us most of the time. One night while I was away, Susie had been sound asleep when all of a sudden she woke with a start. "What was that?" she gasped. A rat had vomited on her but had escaped. How had it got in? Grabbing her flashlight, she searched all around the bed. At the foot she discovered a little hole where the net had not been tucked in properly. From then on she made sure it was tucked in all the way.

One evening just after sunset we heard a great deal of excitement in the open-air kitchen right next to us. I went out to investigate, and immediately a powerful stench stung my nostrils. A hunter had brought in a monkey that he had shot, and the women were burning off all the hair. Then they laid the monkey on the ground and opened up his belly. Everyone began to grab. The law stated that the guts were free for the taking. A lot of confusion resulted as the people fought over the innards. Suddenly a great cry arose.

"Where is the monkey?" everyone shouted. In the darkness and confusion the monkey had disappeared. The people sniffed the air, and the scent of the burned monkey led right to my storeroom, which was closed.

"Teachah Gantah, please open the door," they said. "The monkey is inside there."

"Now how would it get in there?" I scoffed.

"Please just open the door. We can smell it," they insisted. I opened the door, and sure enough, there it was, hidden right behind my barrel. The little houseboy whom the chief had given me for Susie to train had picked it up, raced lickety-split to my storeroom and hidden it there. I thought his actions might create an international incident, but when the villagers had recovered their monkey, all was well.

Our dining room was only about 8 x 8 feet and had one little window. The wood cookstove was just beyond the door in another even smaller room. The heat from that stove and the tropical air, plus 100 percent humidity, was really too much for us. One day at the big Roberts Airport, I got a lot of bearings and parts from a B-27 plane that had crashed. Back in Zondo, I built things out of the parts and finally came up with a quite good hand-operated fan. My little houseboy enjoyed cranking this fan for us while we ate, and it greatly helped to relieve the extreme heat in that small room.

I Flew a Lancaster Bomber

While I was waiting for some parts at Roberts Airport, the British men taking aerial photographs for a map of Liberia asked me if I would like to go along. I eagerly agreed and said, "We will be flying near our station. Could we drop a letter to my wife, perhaps in a big box in your bomb compartment?"

"Why yes," they replied, "that would be fun." We got airborne in that big bird and approached our mission station, but the pilot could not see our place because it was hidden behind the tall trees.

"Let me take the controls, and I will fly you directly over the station," I offered.

He agreed, and when he saw the station, he said, "Let me have it now." He took that big plane and began to whip it around in a circle and lined it up with our 600-foot landing strip. Then he opened up the bomb compartment and dropped the box right onto the airstrip.

When I got back, Susie told me what had happened. "The people had just come out of a church service. When they heard the roar of the four-engine bomber and saw that big plane coming right toward them, they got so scared that they jumped into the jungle." Even the missionaries became scared. But when Susie saw the belly of the plane open and the box come tumbling down, she said, "Oh, Abe must be in that big plane."

We went on to take the photos. Then on the way home those guys tried to scare me. They shut down one engine and feathered the prop. Soon they shut down another and another, until we had only one engine running on the far end of the left wing. I just sat there.

When they saw I wasn't scared, they began to turn on the engines, one at a time. When we got back to Roberts Airport, they asked me, "Weren't you scared?"

"No," I answered. "I was ready to die, but I don't know about you guys."

The Fire God

A certain family made a lot of trouble for the mission at Suakoko. Just down the hill through a little valley in sight of the mission, this family had built a small house. Continually they opposed us, but we prayed for God's name to be glorified. We had moved down to Zondo by then, but I had flown in late on Saturday and was sleeping alone in a house that overlooked the valley and this family's house.

That night a terrible thunderstorm passed over the mission, and lightning struck all over. At the peak of the storm a bolt of lightning hit, such as I had never felt before. It shook the whole area. I knew it had hit down in the valley. As I raised myself on my elbow to look out the window, I could see a small flame coming from the top of the house there. In seconds the whole house was full of fire. I could see one lonely figure darting back and forth in front of the fiery windows. Soon the thatched roof fell in. When I rushed over, I saw eight charred people lying dead where they had slept. The ten-year-old girl had been sleeping on a camp cot that insulated her from the electric shock. Only she escaped. What a sad experience! Two Scripture passages came to my mind: "Be not deceived; God is not mocked . . ." (Gal. 6:7), and "Our God is a consuming fire" (Heb. 12:29).

The work at Suakoko was difficult and slow for many years. The chief, though openly friendly to us, opposed us behind our backs. Then one day he became ill and died. After his death, one of his wives spread the word that he had come to her in a dream. He told her to tell all the people that we missionaries were preaching the truth and that they must all follow God's way. Then things began to change.

Darrell Nearly Drowned

Our son Darrell had just turned three years old when we moved into our first house built on the Zondo station. It had a thatched roof and pole and mud walls (which we whitewashed), but we also had a cement floor, screens on the windows and even a fireplace! Susie was good at making it look beautiful inside. Thus we had our first home, cozy and homey, though it was just a mud shack.

Every day the native schoolboys would run past our house, through the jungle and over a log on the river. Then they would "splash" down into the river. Darrell just loved those black boys. One day, unbeknownst to us, he decided to follow them. All went well until he stepped on the wet slippery log with his leather shoes. Down he went into the river. But God was there and had placed a thorn bush in the river to catch him. Half submerged in water, Darrell began to struggle and scream, but the bush held him. The boys heard him, pulled him out of the water and brought him to the house, sopping wet. They said, "Missy, we found your son caught in the thorn bush on the side of the river." Susie gasped and took him, wet as he was, into her arms and hugged him.

"Oh God," she prayed silently, "You spared him, so we know You have a great plan for his life. Thank You!" The Lord is so good!

The Piper Cub Swallowed by a Storm

When Lud Zerbe replaced me as pilot, I decided he needed a map. Amazingly, our three main stations—Suakoko, Zondo and Tappi—happened to lie in an almost perfect triangle. With all my figures and notes of distances in minutes and degrees of flight between stations and Monrovia, I filled in the details: the other stations, the rivers, the few roads and the coastline. It all resulted in a rather accurate map. The American Geodetic Society even took it and made many copies for all the pilots in Liberia.

Before I got to know the country, I more or less had to feel my way around. I had made the flight from Tappi to Zondo once before and hit it almost on the nose, so I knew my compass heading but did not know the hills that would later become my "friends" (landmarks). On this my second flight, I was bringing Bob Smith from Tappi, where he had recovered from another illness under the wonderful care of Catherine Mellish.

About halfway to Zondo, a great black rain and windstorm loomed in my path. I dared not go off course to skirt around it, for I might get lost. In fact, my gas supply forced me to go straight through it. The sky grew unusually dark in that storm, with the heavy rain pelting my windshield and the wind tossing the little Piper Cub like a cork in a wild ocean. Bob had a favorite expression picked up from the native people: "Ji ji waa," which literally means, "Look out!" As we were being whipped up and down, I heard him say, "Ji ji waa!" And when we plunged down, he would whistle shrilly. I could tell he was scared, and so was I. When I was scared, I would remain quiet, but did I pray!

After what seemed like an eternity, we broke out into beautiful sunshine. Immediately I knew where we were, but Bob did not. Just ahead of us was Gay Peter mission station, with a nice wide path leading to the houses. When Bob saw it, he exclaimed, "Abe, can you set it down there?"

"Bob, look to your left. Do you see the two little hills? That is Zondo. Why don't we go home instead?" He heartily agreed, so I dipped my wing to the left, took up my course and, passing our friendly hills, swung around for a happy landing.

"Boy," Bob commented, "this landing strip is worth all the sweat and money we poured into it!" I agreed. Zondo had become a great center and eventually the base from which we flew into twenty-four other airstrips in our Bassa tribe alone. In all of Liberia we eventually had about sixty airfields.

Harriet Almost Died!

The aviation ministry in Liberia, which Harlan Rahilly and I started, was a bit slow going at first. But when all the stations had been linked by a network of airfields, things became interesting. Then Harlan married Harriet O'Keefe, who was deathly afraid of airplanes and flying, so he left all the flying to me. He and Harriet walked two days into the jungle and started a new station in an extremely heathen village. From time to time I dropped mail and supplies to them in front of their house. I got pretty sharp at it, even bouncing one load right onto their piazza (porch).

A big leopard began snooping around their house at night, so Harlan determined to get him. One night he tied a chicken by the legs, laid it right in front of his house in the moonlight, sat down on the piazza with his shotgun in hand and waited for him. It took a while, but eventually Harlan heard something move and faintly saw the animal. He was *big!* Switching on his hunting light, Harlan could see him in all his splendor with all his beautiful spots. He hesitated just a moment and then pulled the trigger. The shotgun blasted, and the leopard roared. Harriet was in the house nearly dying of fright, thinking the leopard had attacked Harlan. But Harlan had shot well, and the leopard slowly rolled over and died.

About a year later, Harriet became extremely ill. Harlan rounded up some carriers and evacuated her to Suakoko. It was a difficult trip. By the time they arrived, her condition was grave. Mrs. Mellish, our senior nurse, had somehow appeared at Suakoko. Then the Lord led me to fly there at just the right time too, for we had no radios then. The J3 Cub could carry only one passenger.

"If we don't get her to Monrovia today, she will never make it," Mrs. Mellish warned. "We need ice to treat her fever, and we don't have any here."

"Let's go, Catherine," I said. "I will take you down first and then come back for Harriet."

This incident occurred during the rainy season, but I had learned to fly through such weather. In an hour and a half we were circling Monrovia and buzzing the mission house so the missionaries would come to meet us. Swinging over the Army drill field, I came in for a smooth three-point landing. The soldiers cooperated nicely, but after I shut off the engine, the general came over, looking stern. Saluting me, he asked, "Captain, who gave you permission to land on my drill field?"

"The president of Liberia, sir!" I assured him, saluting back.

"Then you are OK," he responded, relaxing. I thanked him.

"I have a sick missionary to bring on my next flight. May I come in again this afternoon, sir?"

"Yes, you may," he replied. I thanked him and, leaving Catherine with the missionaries that had come for her, I took off.

The rain was heavy, but I dodged the worst of the downpours and made it back to Suakoko. Harlan helped me gas up in the rain, using an umbrella to catch most of the rain. The rest was trapped in the chamois skin through which we filtered all our gas. He asked no questions about the weather. He knew as well as I that only by the grace of God would I be able to get through the clouds that hung on the trees and the steam and fog that rose out of the jungle. The carriers brought Harriet in a hammock. When she was comfortably settled in the backseat, Harlan flipped the prop for me. After checking my instruments and praying for safety, I took off again into the "soup."

Harriet seemed relaxed and didn't know the battle I had to fight for the next hour. Hopping from tree to tree, through clouds and fog, I fought desperately to hold onto visual contact with the trees but not fly into them. Then the terrain dropped 500 feet, and I had to drop down with it. I sweated and struggled to keep between the trees and clouds. Finally the ceiling lifted a bit, and I was able to relax and cruise into Monrovia. Again I dipped my right wing over the Army field, slipped over the huts and then flew straight in, greasing my wheels down on that welcome, smooth, grassy drill field. Catherine was waiting. She took care of a very sick Harriet. Harlan came down soon on a money-bus, got tickets for a Pan Am flight and flew home to America with Harriet, who soon recovered. We again gave thanks unto the Lord for that little airplane called, "The Good News."

A New House

We made thousands of mud blocks, baked them in the sun and began to build another, bigger house at Zondo. I laid the first layer of sun-dried mud blocks in a mortar of mud upon a foundation of rock and mud. I covered that with strips of sheet metal soldered together so the termites would be unable to go into our walls and eat our woodwork. I taught the schoolboys to lay the blocks, and soon the walls were up. We used wooden poles for rafters and aluminum sheeting I had flown in for a roof. (I fixed a special saddle for the roofing to ride in, on the outside of the plane.)

Did that roof ever shine in the tropical sun! People came walking for days just to see this beautiful sight in the heart of the jungle. Once, some time later, Lud Zerbe flew home above a thin layer of fog, spotted the glare of that roof and landed safely.

Because cement had to be flown in from a hundred miles away, we used it sparingly for the floors only. Finally we moved in. While we were building, the people came around commenting, "Thank you, yet" (congratulations on progress thus far). But after we had finished the house, they said, "Thank you, yah!" (congratulations). The chief and others came to look through the house, so we gave them all a grand tour.

I Apologize, Chief!!

Tony, the aircraft mechanic from Roberts Airport, came to spend Christmas with us. He loved the things of God, and we enjoyed him. On Christmas Day we had a good time in the church with our people. Afterward, we shared a feast with the believers.

In the afternoon the village chief brought four of the town elders to visit with us. While we chatted on the porch, I excused myself, went into the kitchen and loaded a plate with Christmas goodies. When I came out, I went right down the line, giving each man a sweet. The chief stood at the end of the line. When I offered him some, he became angry, stood up in a huff and walked away with all his men following behind munching on the Christmas goodies.

I was stunned! Tony remarked, "What a stupid guy. Stupid, stupid!!"

I replied, "No, Tony, you and I don't understand something here. Let's go ask our native pastor."

When I told the pastor what had happened, he exclaimed, "Oh! Teachah Gantah, you really did it that time. You made the chief out to be the small boy by serving him last of all. You should have given the plate to him first and let him serve his men."

"Oh, I see. Let me go to the chief and apologize."

I walked into the village, a five minutes' walk from our house. I went right to the chief's house and said, "Chief, I am so sorry for what I did to you today. I have so many good things yet to learn from you, and I am sorry for the way I shamed you in front of your men today. Please forgive me!"

He was amazed to see me humble myself before him. The nationals themselves had told me to my face that I was "much greater" than the president of Liberia himself and that whatever I told the president to do, he had to do. My humbling myself before the chief had an amazing effect on them all. "He that humbleth himself shall be exalted" (Luke 14:11), and I was exalted among them for that.

Fire!

The Lud Zerbes arrived to replace us so we could go on our first furlough. They moved into our old house until we could leave for furlough; then they would move into our new house. In the old house, with its mud walls and thatched roof, the smoke from the woodstove rose right into the attic, killing the bugs that otherwise would have destroyed the roof.

One Monday night we had gathered in our new house for prayer meeting time. We had just finished our Bible study and visiting when, just before we closed our eyes for prayer, we saw a great light burst into the black African sky outside. We quickly ran outside and saw that the whole roof of our old house was on fire. The Zerbes' two children were sleeping in the house, so we all ran in one door, through the house and out the other, carrying children and anything else we could grab. The fiery thatch fell down onto the palm-mat ceilings. Nevertheless, we kept racing through the house, salvaging what we could until the rafters started coming down. The fire burned through the mats, and the whole roof caved in between the mud walls. But we had saved the children and most of the Zerbes' belongings, praise God!

The next morning young Lesley Zerbe asked, "Daddy, where are my glasses?" He was almost blind without them, so we all went outside to look for them. We were sure they had burned in the fire. However, on searching around in the grass, we found them! In all the excitement and tramping around, God had kept them from being destroyed. What a wonderful, caring God we have!

A Bad Seed; A Good Seed

After our first furlough we brought back a few things to make our house more comfortable. One day I entered my office and was shocked to find a big hole in the cement floor. The thought flashed through my mind, "Who did that?" But as I looked more closely, I noticed that my own mistake had caused the hole. When I poured the floor, I had unknowingly mixed a small seed in with the cement. That little seed took its time until one day it began to grow and push and then burst my cement floor wide open.

That seed reminded me of an incident that took place when I was newly saved. I wanted everyone to know the wonderful new life I had found in Christ. But how could I get my neighbors to listen? An idea came to me. I ordered a lot of garden seeds, then hitched my little bronco to the sleigh and, going from house to house, sold the seeds. After a sale, I would lay a gospel tract on top of the sale and say, "This is the seed of the Word of God, and it is free."

On our first furlough home from Africa, one of my old neighbors, Mr. Abe Neudorf, came up to me after a service.

"Abe, do you remember some years ago coming to my farm and selling garden seeds? You put a tract on top of the seeds. I was so angry that day, I almost hit you with my fist. Then my sister died, and God began to speak to me: 'You will have to die, too, someday.' I remembered the tract and read it again and again. And the Lord wonderfully saved me. Thank you so much! I am so happy. My whole family is saved now. My boys are even preparing to be missionaries."

God has promised His Word will not return unto Him void. The seed of a tree is powerful, but the seed of the Word of God is all-powerful! Praise God!

The Devil Society Pulls In Its Horns

One time when Bob Smith and I spent the night at the Firestone Rubber Plantation, a disaster occurred back in Zondo village. As soon as we landed home, Susie came running from the village and told us that the Devil Society's big leaders had met the previous night and that morning and had decided that all the Christians must leave the village. They also decided to banish Pastor Gaye from the area.

Bob was a tall man with a powerful voice and a commanding presence. Most of the natives stood only as tall as his armpit. As we walked into the village, we faced the leaders of the Devil Society and asked them if what we had heard were really so. Then we told them that if it were so, we would turn right around with our airplane to go to Monrovia and tell the president what was going on here. They looked at one another, afraid, and began to back down. They gave permission for the pastor to stay and for all the Christians to stay too. They made a complete turnaround. The Christians began to clap their hands; then they broke into singing and followed the singing with prayers of praise for a great deliverance.

Another village, one hour's walk from Zondo, was also persecuting the believers. Word reached us, so Lud Zerbe and I decided to go and bombard the village with nose dives and a lot of noise from the airplane. It worked. The airplane had become so many things: a door opener, a means of gaining favor with the government officials when we flew them around occasionally, and an encouragement and help to the believers.

Kronemeyer Opens Krahn

Walter Kronemeyer, on leaving Tappi one day, declared, "Abe, I am walking over to the Krahn tribe to build an airstrip. When I have finished it, I will send a runner to bring you word." In about two weeks, a runner came with a letter.

"Abe, come," the letter said. "We are ready for you. Bring my wife and daughter."

I couldn't believe it! How could Walt have built an airstrip so quickly? But I obeyed, and since it was a sunny day, I flew high so that I could see far, for the airstrip would be another needle in a haystack to find. Old Baldy, the mountain with a lone tree gracing its rounded crest, was a good landmark, so I headed right over it and kept going. After about 15 minutes over that emerald jungle with nothing in sight but high forest, I spotted a clearing ahead. I let down for a "look see." I had found it!

I saw Walt standing there with a lot of black people all looking up at me and waving. But the airstrip . . . ! "No, Walt, no way! That is no airstrip; it is much too short," I protested silently. Still I kept circling and looking at him. I saw that he had his hands together in a praying attitude, and that kind of put the pressure on me. However, I remembered the verse the Lord had given me right at the beginning of my flying in Liberia: "Thou shalt not tempt the Lord thy God" (Matt. 4:7).

"Abe, you must not take chances," I thought. "Let me see. . . . It might help if I fly across the bottom end of the strip to see if it runs uphill." When I looked, I saw it had quite an uphill slant to it, so I made a trial approach for a landing. Then I knew I could make it in. I gunned the throttle and went around again. As I made my final approach, I slipped it gently, set the wheels down right at the end and rolled up the hill to an easy stop. Immediately all those wonderful people surrounded the plane.

Walt instantly responded, "Let us praise God and give thanks to His wonderful Name!" Another door had been opened to another tribe for the gospel.

On one of my next flights there, I had a big load of supplies. I spotted a woman coming from my right with a big load on her head and a baby on her back. I was committed to a landing, and I was sure she would stop. But she was deaf and dumb and kept on coming. Then, out of the corner of her eye, she spotted the plane and got scared. She began to run right in front of me to the village, the only place of safety. I quickly applied full power and, pulling back on the stick, I barely cleared her. The tall trees that had not yet been cut down at the end of the field came rushing at me. I kept the stick forward to build up maximum speed, and I prayed: "Oh Lord! I like that verse in Your Book that says, 'Underneath are the everlasting arms' [Deut. 33:27]. I need them now, Lord!" And with that, I pulled back on the stick, shooting almost straight up. As I went over the trees, I could feel the plane going into a stalling shudder, but it cleared. My knees shook, so I took a wide sweep in a circle before landing safely with a heartfelt "Thank You, God!"

Look Out—Elephants!

The church at Zondo had gone through a time of persecution that had made the believers strong, and it was a joy to work with those dear people. One of the young men came to me one day.

"Teachah, three days' walk from here" (pointing with his chin as the people always do), "there is a village called Goah Town. It is too wicked! They have refused the missionaries and the gospel."

Later a government tax collector told me that officials were afraid to go to Goah Town. One day when he was there, the people had nearly killed him by their witchcraft. They had thrown lightning at him, and a ball of fire rolled right through the open kitchen, just missing him.

"I will never go back!" he said to me. "They are wicked too much!"

"I want to go and visit them," I announced. "Who will go with me?"

Four strong young men immediately responded. "We want to go with you," they said. So we prepared and left.

The sun shone brightly, and the temperature was hot. The high, thick jungle created a shaded canopy that kept the path quite pleasant. We arrived at one village and were shocked to find that smallpox had smitten the whole town. The people were dying like flies. What could we do? We had no medicine, but why not preach to them? There we stood between the living and dying and held out to them the Word of Life. No doubt we will meet some of them in Glory someday.

After an hour back on the trail, we heard something big crashing through the trees. "What's that?" I whispered. The young men answered in hushed tones.

"Teachah Gantah—elephants! Look, there are fresh droppings. Let's get out of here!" We began to run, for my .22 caliber rifle was no match for an elephant.

When we got a safe distance away, the trees suddenly filled with monkeys. One of the men asked, "Please, Teachah, would you bring down one for us?" I looked straight up; and there, perhaps 200 feet above me, I saw a red monkey breast glowing in the sun. I took careful aim and pulled the trigger. Down he came, straight for my head. I took one step back, and he dropped right in front of me. Was he ever big— perhaps weighing 35 pounds! The men were so happy they began to dance and thank me over and over. Then one spoke up again.

"Teachah, if you could shoot one more, we could take it into the village, trade it for rice and have one great feast tonight."

"I will try," I agreed, and began to look for another monkey, not paying too much attention to where I was stepping.

Suddenly the man behind me screamed, "Look out!" I jumped and then looked back.

"What is the matter?" I demanded.

"Didn't you see that green mamba snake go right between your legs?"

"No," I replied, "I was looking for monkeys." He wagged his finger in my face.

"Teachah Gantah, you should be more careful. When that snake bites you, you have only five minutes to live."

"Maybe you fellows should walk ahead of me, and I will follow," I suggested.

The sun was dropping low over the jungle by the time we arrived in Goah Town. We had to present ourselves to the chief. He had on a long flowing gown and an elephant's tail in his hand. He sat on his piazza and was surprised to see a white man coming toward him. I shook hands with him and, snapping his fingers together with mine, I said, "Moin." (Have you slept well?)

"Aye, moin," he responded. (Yes, I have slept well.)

"I am Gantah," I said, by way of introduction. Then he really came to life. The people had given me that version of my name, Guenter, and by then it had spread all through the jungles as the name of the man in the "iron bird." It did not matter if it were a bomber, a Pan Am Clipper or the Piper Cub; they were all "Gantah" to them. They always gave their babies meaningful names. If a plane happened to fly over a village when a baby was born, his parents called him Gantah. A whole crop of Gantahs is growing up over there.

The chief then asked me, "Gantah, can you make your iron bird fall down in my town?"

"Yes," I replied, "if you will fix me a place."

"We will do it," he exclaimed excitedly. "We will do it, but you must show us how." I asked the men to pull some of those strong vines out of the tall trees and bring them to me. I tied them together into a 100-foot measuring line.

"Chief," I said, "you must cut a wide road in the jungle long enough to lay this line down ten times." Some of the men had been to the Firestone Rubber Plantation and knew what a straight road looked like, but most of them had never seen anything straight, because their paths, rivers, trees and even some houses were crooked.

"My people are strong," the chief replied. "We will do it for you."

After a few more days of our preaching, these "wicked people" became excited about a new life and a new hope for the future. We went home then, and they went right to work. Before long, the chief's messenger, wearing a red cap with a gold star on it, appeared at my door in Zondo. He saluted me and reported, "Airport finished, sir," and gave me the letter from the chief. I was amazed but flew over there, covering in 15 minutes the distance that had taken us three days to walk. I saw they had really done a fantastic job, but the trees were still tall on both ends of the field. So I put the control stick between my knees as I circled and wrote a letter to the chief.

"Dear Chief,

Thank you for your good work, but would you
please cut the trees on both ends of the field?"

Then I crumpled the letter in my hand, and flying low right past the chief, I threw it out. The wind caught it and opened it up nicely so that it fluttered down right at the chief's feet.

A few days later I flew back. Sure enough, they had cleared away the trees on both ends of the field. I came down low and slow to look the field over, but I was disappointed. The tall termite anthills had only been spread out, so there were humps all over the field. I went around again, trying to find one short smooth place where I could perhaps put my wheels down and squeeze in for a landing. By the third pass over the field, a crowd had gathered where the path came from the village.

I picked a place. I came around for the fourth time. Then slowly, with the flaps on, I slipped the plane gently, dropped on the spot I had chosen and skidded to a stop. Then a great wave of people rolled toward me and, with excitement and shouting, surrounded the plane. Everybody wanted to shake my hand and snap my fingers. One big fat woman actually hugged me! Then the chief came and welcomed me and thanked me in his stately way.

I guided the men in leveling the runway, which resulted in another open door for the gospel. On a regular basis we began to have clinics with preaching, and the Lord blessed with many souls turning to Him. Before long, we had a church going.

The church there became a center for outreach. The Lord raised up a leader among them called Waya. He developed into a godly pastor and a good preacher, and the people loved him dearly.

One day Waya became ill. His wife, Tee Tee, did all she could to make him well again. "Tee Tee," he said, "you have been so good and kind, but I won't need any more food or medicine. I have seen Heaven and Jesus, and He says I must come now." She began to cry and pleaded for him to eat and take his medicine. Instead he said, "Go call all the believers now so I can pray with them and say good-bye." With a heavy and troubled heart she went.

When the believers had gathered around him, he admonished them to be strong and to let their lights shine for Jesus. "Don't make a heathen funeral for me with death wails, rolling on the ground and pulling out of hair, but show the heathen the Christian way—that we are not without hope." Then he exclaimed, "Here He comes! Good-bye," and he went to Glory. This witness and funeral shook the whole village and the whole area!

Our nurse, Joan Peckinpaugh, with her great nursing ability and kind manner, was a great blessing to the people of Goah Town too. Once we went to preach on a Sunday, and the people showed me a woman who had been shot in the shoulder by her own husband. Her bones were exposed; it was a terrible sight. We made our service short, then flew her out for medical help. She lived. News of this event had a way of filtering through the jungles; consequently, airstrips sprung up all over. What a great tool the airplane had become!

The Bush Cow Tragedy

One day I flew out to preach and, landing on a grassy field near the ocean, I rolled to a stop near a village. When I shut off the engine and opened the cockpit door, I heard great screaming and wailing and saw people rolling on the ground. The death wail pierced the air around me. Even the chief, who usually was quite sedate, came running to me and cried, "Oh Teachah Gantah! Oh Teachah Gantah!" with tears streaming down his cheeks. When I asked him what was the matter, he just kept wailing, obviously beside himself, and crying, "Oh Teachah Gantah! Oh Teachah Gantah!"

"Please tell me what happened!" I begged. Finally he spoke.

"My brother, my brother . . . he went into the bush [jungle] to shoot a bush cow. When he pulled the trigger, the gun went off, but the bullet missed the wild cow. The bush cow gored him and pinned him down with its sharp horns. Now he is dying. Oh my brother! Oh my brother!"

"Let's go and see him," I urged. The tragedy had happened a few days before, and as I entered the mud hut, I could smell him, for gangrene had set in. When I entered his room, he looked at me from his grass mat on the floor.

"Teachah Gantah, will you save me?" he pleaded weakly, lifting up his feeble arms. It struck me that here was a perfect picture of every lost sinner: helpless, hopeless, his sin a stench in the nostrils of God, and on his way to sure destruction. Yet the ear of God is always open to hear the cry of every lost sinner, just as mine was open to this man's plea for help. "Whosoever shall call upon the name of the Lord shall be saved" (Rom. 10:13).

"Yes, I will try," I said, but I was so glad that God never has to say He will *try,* for "he is able also to save them to the uttermost that come unto God by him . . ." (Heb. 7:25).

Some men carried him to the plane in a hammock. I eased him into the back seat of the Piper Cub and strapped him in. The plane had no starter, so I put my left foot in front of the right tire and flipped the prop with my right hand. The engine came to life. I jumped into the cockpit and poured the power to her. As the wheels began to spin down the grassy strip, I pulled back on the stick, and we took off. We pulled up through the fleecy clouds and cruised smoothly to a gentle landing at Roberts Airport. Then in a Liberian truck we bounced 15 miles down the road to the Firestone Rubber Plantation hospital. When the doctor saw me, he asked, "Abe, what did you bring me today?"

"Nothing good," I replied. "In fact, something very bad, but would you try to help him, please?"

"Yes, of course we will try," he agreed.

"Thanks, Doc!" I said as I left. Time passed until one day a native runner came from Firestone. "Teachah Gantah, that sick man is coming along small small" (a little). More time passed, and I somewhat forgot about the incident until my first landing at Trade Town, the village where people used to trade off the natives they had captured in tribal warfare. Arab traders would pay them $15 per person. The Africans were then shipped to America as slaves. The name had stuck, and here was a new era opening up for Trade Town. A Piper Cub had opened it up to a new world and the gospel.

As I rolled in for the first landing, people came running and shouting with great joy. They all wanted to feel the plane and shake hands and snap fingers with Teachah Gantah. My finger was getting tired and sore, but along came another man. He hung onto my hand and wouldn't let go. Looking into my eyes, he said, "Teachah Gantah, don't you know me?" I knew I had seen him somewhere, but where? He finally pulled up his T-shirt and showed me the bush cow wounds, now healed. Then I remembered.

"Zoga, you didn't die?" I exclaimed, grabbing his hand again.

"No, Teachah Gantah. You saved me!" Then he put his hand deep into his pocket and pulled out a fifty-cent piece. He looked a bit embarrassed as he faced me again. "Teachah Gantah, would you take this for your airplane? It is all I have. Thank you for saving me."

Something clicked in my mind. Somewhere I had read that if our bodies were reduced to the elements they contain, they would be worth about fifty cents, maybe a dollar. What a picture! He was giving me his *all*. The Bible says, "I beseech you therefore, brethren, by the mercies of God, that ye present your bodies a living sacrifice, holy, acceptable unto God, which is your reasonable service" (Rom. 12:1).

"If Jesus Christ be God and died for me, then no sacrifice can be too great that I can make for Him" (C. T. Studd).

Bob Shoots a Bush Cow

Bush cows were wild, vicious and dangerous and were a menace to the native people's farms. When they got into a rice farm, they would destroy most of it in short order. The villagers liked to tell a story about a big native woman who saw a bush cow on her farm, sneaked up to him, with both hands grabbed onto his big horns and held his head down. (A bush cow has little strength to lift up his head if it is held down.) She put her full weight on the head, forcing it down to the ground while hollering for help. Her husband came running and, with several whacks of his machete, cut the animal's head right off. The rejoicing and feasting that followed were something else!

One day some Christians came running to Bob Smith in great excitement and begged, "Teachah Smith, please bring your big gun. There is a bush cow in our farm!" With great haste he grabbed his Savage 300 rifle and followed them. When the bull saw the people coming, he slipped into the swordgrass. (It clings to you and will cut you severely if you pull away; but if you take your time and pull it up slowly, you can free yourself from it.) They began to follow the bush cow carefully along the path it had made, dodging the swordgrass as they went. Two men prowled ahead of Bob, and one crept behind as they proceeded stealthily. Suddenly the lead man cried:

"Look out! Here he comes!" He dodged the oncoming horns. The second man jumped onto the bull's horns and, leaping up, grabbed for a tree. Bob was next in line. At the last moment, he dodged to the right and fired his gun as the bull flashed by. The fourth man got knocked down, but the bull spun around and came back for the man with the gun. Bob saw him coming and shot him right through his thick skull. For good measure Bob pumped two more bullets into him as he fell down and breathed his last. Sad to say, the man who was knocked down died later. So triumph turned into tragedy and great sadness that day.

Later Bob shot another bush cow. Since we had no refrigeration in those days, I flew part of it to the chef at the Roberts Airport mess hall. He was delighted to buy it and debated, "Now, let's see; what will I call this on the menu? Oh yes! I will call it, 'Liberian buffalo steak!' "

Chief Dabapa Died

One Sunday after church I was told that Chief Dabapa was very ill, so after lunch I took some medicine with me and walked the hour to go to see him. I found him outside his village in a little shelter that the villagers had built for him. He had a high fever and was very ill indeed. I treated him for malaria, talked to him again about the Lord, prayed with him and went home. He died the next day.

The chief had claimed to be a man who in spirit could go into an alligator. His special alligator was extremely large. The chief told his hunter never to shoot alligators in the big river. One day the hunter and his "small boy" (young assistant) were out hunting when they saw some alligators sunning themselves on the rocks in the river. The hunter prepared to shoot.

"The chief told you not to shoot alligators here," the young fellow reminded him.

"When I see meat, I have to shoot." Bang! He had aimed at the biggest one, and his aim was good. The huge reptile slipped into the water. A lot of blood came up, but the alligator had disappeared, so the hunter and his small boy returned to the village.

"Did you shoot an alligator?" the chief called. The hunter denied it. The chief insisted, "But you did, and it was my alligator." Then the chief became ill, and in a few days he died.

The people explained to me that the chief died because he was in the alligator. "Now they both died." The Africans claimed that if a person were in an animal when it got wounded, the person would become ill. Then when the animal died, the human would have to die with it.

The next morning I walked back to the village. The villagers had already buried the chief. They had dug a six-foot hole in the middle of his hut, then at a right angle a long ten-foot tunnel. First, they pushed his body all the way to the end. Next, they took all his belongings, pushed them in behind him and then filled the hole with dirt. They lit a lantern, which they set on his grave, and two men kept watch day and night. They were not going to let any spirits find the chief's body and carry it away. I did not understand this custom and still don't.

Some time before Chief Dabapa died, many people had disappeared from that area. While they crossed the river in a canoe, "leopard people" grabbed them, pulled them under the water, cut their hearts out (for a sacrifice to their gods) and left the corpses. These "leopard people" would dress in leopard skins and put on claws of steel with which they grabbed their victims. Finally the chief called the big witch doctor to find out which men in his village were the leopard people. The big man came, mixed up some brew and made the suspected people drink his concoction. Then they had to stand in a long line in the hot sun. After about ten minutes, two of the men began to weave around and then fell straight down on their faces. The witch doctor said, "There you have your men." How can the Devil fight against the Devil?

Pastor Is Dying!

"Teachah Gantah, quick read this!" the runner cried, as he emerged from the jungle and thrust a letter into my hand. Pastor Dennis had written it.

"Teachah Gantah, I am dying with strangulated hernia. If you don't come today, it will be too late."

I always kept my airplane gassed up and ready, so the messenger and I flew out over the jungle. In seven minutes we greased in for a landing and rolled to a stop in front of the pastor's house. Some men brought him out in a hammock. He was in great agony, and every move produced cries of pain. After a word of prayer we were airborne, heading straight to Monrovia.

The flight took an hour, and the late afternoon turned to sunset as we approached the capital city. The city had no airfield, but over the hill from all the different embassies, right beside the ocean, was a rock quarry that had been smoothed out for us pilots. I circled. My friend saw me, came out and took us to the hospital.

Things were primitive and informal then, so while we waited for the doctor to come, I actually shaved the man on his bed, helping to prepare him for the operation. When the doctor came, he exclaimed, "My, oh my! We must get to work right away," and he did. After he had finished operating, he told me, "If you had not brought him in today, he would have been a goner."

Five days later I flew Pastor Dennis home. The church people there were so thankful to have him back. One of them commented, "This church can't play—o," meaning "We really mean business for the Lord."

Teachah, I Can Walk Again!

In those early days, as I flew around and saw so many sick people, I was profoundly burdened for them. We had a few nurses, but because they were loaded down with the daily large crowds that came to the stations, I learned how to give injections. Giving out fever pills and aspirins was easy, of course. I would preach on Sunday in three places, then backtrack on Monday mornings to take medicine to the sick.

We often saw a tropical disease called yaws. The victim would break out in red sores all over his body. But with a few cheap injections, the disease would clear up. The patients would cover my medical costs by giving me rice, bananas, pineapples or even a few pennies. They were truly thankful for the great help I gave them.

One man who lived in "Little Cola" had not walked for years, and the muscles in his legs had shrunk until they were useless. I treated him, prayed for him and told him he was going to walk again, with the help of God. Before I left, I instructed the family to build a fence that the man could hold onto to lift himself to his feet and help him walk.

Three weeks later when I returned, the man excitedly exclaimed, "Teachah Gantah, I can walk again; you just watch me now." He grabbed hold of the fence, lifted himself and, though his legs shook and wobbled, slowly began to follow that fence, holding onto it. Soon afterward he could walk by himself, even work in his farm. Was it a miracle? Yes! All healings are miracles of God, for all healing must come from Him. "I am the Lord that healeth thee" (Exod. 15:26).

The Devil's Chief Dies

One day the chief of the Devil Society died in Zondo. The throbbing sounds of loud drums went right through us all night. Though we lived a quarter of a mile from the village, we hardly slept that night due to the din. The next morning I walked into the village. The whole place was full of a sickening smell from the dead body. I went to our chief and expressed my sympathies.

"No, he is not dead," the chief explained. "He has just gone on a long journey." (They were keeping the body hidden in a hut.)

"Oh," I said politely, "then what is that strong smell?" He just shrugged his shoulders. That night the villagers built a great fire all around the corpse and somewhat cooked it. By morning the smell had gone. They put the body into a coffin made by the native carpenter.

In the afternoon I returned to the village. I could hear the beating of the drums in the secret Devil Bush on the edge of the village. Sometimes I was a bit too bold: I dared to go into the Devil Bush to see for myself, for the chief and I were good friends. When he saw me coming, he became angry and said to his son, who was supposed to watch out for anyone coming, "How is it that you allowed Gantah to come in here?"

"He just walked right by me," the son replied fearfully. To appease the chief's wrath, I spoke up kindly.

"But chief, you are my good friend, and is it so bad for me to come and give you 'never mind' [sympathy] for your dead brother?"

Relenting a little, he said, "Still you must pay a big fine." I had a little change in my pocket, so I gave it to him and the "palaver" [disagreement] was over.

They Butchered a Boy

In 1947 a village near the coast built an airfield. It was barely finished, but I managed to squeeze in for a landing and join many Christians who had gathered for a soul-winning conference. My flying in was an important event, for the airfield was one of the first strips built entirely by the natives.

Many souls were saved, and a church was started. Eventually we organized it into a Baptist church. That was a big day too. Since the people did not have a church bell, I brought a large oxygen welding tank (that had sprung a leak) from the Firestone Rubber Plantation. They put into the ground two poles that were forked on top, and then they tied another one across them. Then we hung the large tank onto the horizontal pole and tried it out for sound. The ring was beautiful, and it carried out far over the jungle to the neighboring villages. I had brought some red paint to make it look beautiful as well, and the church had bought a big new shiny pressure lantern of which they were very proud. It was a great and happy day as the pastor, a Bible school graduate, took over. What a blessing! What a joy!

I kept visiting that church from time to time to encourage and strengthen the believers. On one visit I walked around from house to house just enjoying their fellowship. Then I noticed a ten-pound brass ring, 7 inches across and 1.5 inches thick with four knobs attached to the side. It was half buried in mud, so I pulled it out, cleaned it off and carried it to the deacon next door. "Deacon Carr, please tell me what this is," I requested.

"Oh yes, Teachah Gantah, I will tell you," he replied. "My grandfather was the big chief in this village. He was so afraid of spirits, sicknesses, war and other people's witchcraft that he went to the big, big witch doctor for the most powerful witchcraft he could make. With the help of the blacksmith, they poured this beautifully marked brass ring. The day he brought it, we were all excited. The witch doctor laid the ring down in the middle of the village and attached a cow tail on each knob. Then he asked the men of the village to build a small shelter over it. A group of men went into the jungle with their machetes. They brought back the materials, and they built the roof over it. By then the sun was going down and the witch doctor had a meeting with just the elders of the village and my grandfather. He told them, 'You asked for the most powerful witchcraft, and that always needs a human sacrifice. I want you to bring a young boy at midnight to the new god so we can make this sacrifice.' An eight-year-old boy, with his mouth gagged, was brought that night. They cut his throat and spilled all his blood on the brass ring, and from that time on, all the activities of the village revolved around the 'brass god': sacrifices, worship and all. But when the gospel came, we threw the ring away and turned to the true and living God." The gospel is "the power of God unto salvation to every one that believeth" (Rom. 1:16). Hallelujah!

A Dugout Canoe

In the early '50s, our boys, Wesley and Darrell, spent much time with the native boys. They would even go out into the villages with the boys and preach the gospel. Deacon William declared, "The world is really changing when you see the children preaching God's Word."

One day our boys and some of the mission boys went out into the jungle with axes and cut down a rather large tree. They came back all excited.

"Daddy," they exclaimed, "we're going to make a dugout canoe."

"Great," I said, enthusiastically. "Let's go see." It was a long walk through the forest, and I knew it would be a big, hard job to move that heavy canoe once they got it ready to move.

I encouraged them and challenged them. "When you guys get it to the river, I will give you two dollars," I promised. Then the activity increased! Wesley and Darrell promised the native boys the $2 if and when the canoe reached the water. Every day right after school they were out there hacking away. It took about a month, but the day finally came.

"Daddy, today we are going to bring that canoe to the water." I went with them and witnessed a lot of feverish activity. About fifteen Bassa boys and our two pushed and shoved while rolling the canoe on pieces of logs, bit by bit, until finally, "splash," into the water it went. We all rejoiced in a good job well done and for the lessons learned.

They, together with their native friends, spent many delightful hours playing with the canoe in the water. Bill Thompson, a visiting friend from missionary radio station ELWA, got a bang out of seeing Wesley leaning back leisurely in the boat, with a straw in his mouth, being paddled around. "There goes Tom Sawyer Number Two," he chuckled.

The Witch Doctor a Christian??

After the airport in Trade Town opened, we asked the Christians from the other centers to go there to put on a soul-winning conference. Many of them came. It was the rainy season, a time when most of the people stay in the village. We had services at daybreak, noon and evening. We used the time in between to visit from house to house and to fellowship around the delicious native foods. I had committed myself to eating their food and sleeping in their short native beds, and they liked that.

The church was the same simple mud-wall-and-thatched-roof type of building used everywhere, but it was long. The people filled it from meeting to meeting, and God began to bless His precious Word to their hearts. Many turned to Christ; it was a joyous time. Toward the end of the week, the witch doctor who had also been coming stood up and, lifting his hands, declared, "Today I am ready to believe too. Will you pray for me?" We did and then we really began to rejoice, but one always wonders if a profession is real. You wait to see some fruit.

Three weeks later I returned. As I walked into the village, the young pastor met me and invited me into his house. I wondered what was up when he began to close all the window shutters and the door until it was quite dark in his house. Then he pulled a box from underneath his bed, and turning to me, he whispered, "Teachah Gantah, the witch doctor gave me all his witchcraft." Opening the box, he said, "There it is. He wants you to carry it out of here in your airplane."

The witch doctor had truly turned from idols and witchcraft to serve the true and living God. Praise God!

That day I noticed something different about the village. In a circle around the village stood some large cottonwood trees that almost seemed to guard the village.

"What is the meaning of these tall trees surrounding your village?" I asked. One man explained, telling me this story:

"Many years ago my grandfather went to the witch doctor for some powerful witchcraft to protect this village from sickness, evil spirits and enemies who would shoot fiery arrows onto the thatched roofs. The witch doctor gave him some small trees to plant around the village. Before planting the trees he was told to put a live baby in every hole, cover it up and then plant the tree on top of it."

"Oh no," I exclaimed, horrified.

Someone in America once asked me, "Why don't you leave the happy heathen alone?" But I have not seen any happy heathen. They live their whole lifetimes in fear of spirits, witchcraft, evil spells cast on them by others, and death. In their thinking no one dies naturally; it is always a result of someone bewitching them. We believers have this assurance: "For God hath not given us the spirit of fear; but of power, and of love, and of a sound mind" (2 Tim. 1:7). Truly we have peace that passes understanding.

IT ISN'T FAIR!

It isn't fair! It can't be right!
I now protest with all my might!
I raise my voice both loud and strong.
It's wrong, my friend! It's wrong, it's wrong.

It's wrong, I say, dead wrong, indeed!
That's why I weep and beg and plead.
It is a black and wicked sin
To keep the light from dying men!

I plead the cause of men afar,
Unsaved, unloved, untold they are.
Why have we been so late and slow?
Why have there been so few to go?

Unsaved, unsought and still untold,
Because we love and hoard our gold!
How dare we show such selfish greed
And keep the truth from men in need?

Let's follow Jesus' last command!
Let's take the light to every land!
This truth is plain: the need is great;
The time is short; the hour is late!

Let's not linger, rest or sleep,
But rise and go and give and weep!
And quickly tell a dying race
Of Jesus' love and power and grace!
                                    —*Author Unknown*

First Landing at Zorzor

Ellie Munter, a new missionary, was ill and feared that she had cancer, but we could offer no help. A Lutheran nurse visiting Tappi told me, "Abe, we have a fine doctor up at Zorzor, and I am sure you could land your small airplane on the grass of the government compound there. Why don't you give it a try?"

But where was Zorzor? I would have to feel my way again. Three days from Suakoko by trail would be about 30 minutes flying, so heading in the general direction that was pointed out to me, I took off with a full load of gas. The weather was good, so I climbed high and, as I passed the third ridge, my 30 minutes were up. Below me was the only zinc roof for miles around. The hospital and the large village of Zorzor, with about 200 huts, were spread before me.

I spotted the large grassy compound and made a few approaches

Franz and Suzannah Guenter with son John, daughter Annie and baby Abraham

1947: First plane (J3 Piper) and first hangar—"Pilot Abe"

*Abe in his
Super Cub, 1961*

*Left to right: Susie, Wesley, Darrell
and Abe with little Suzanne in between*

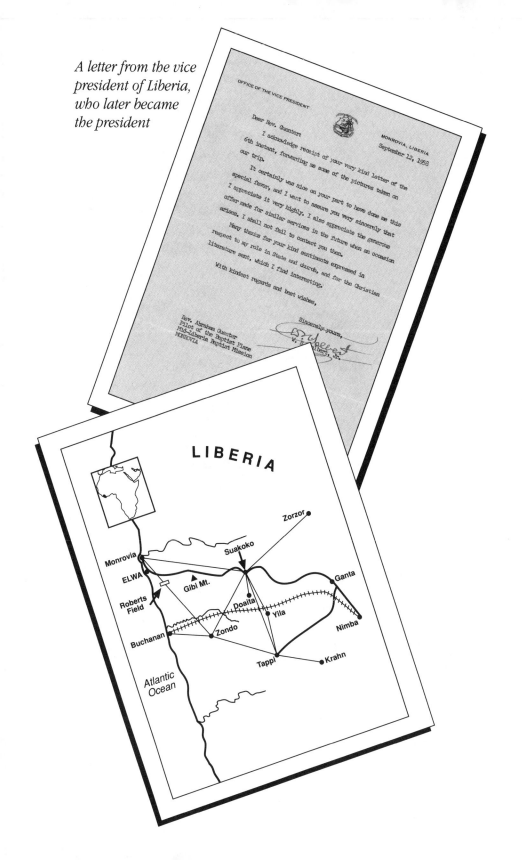

A letter from the vice president of Liberia, who later became the president

OFFICE OF THE VICE PRESIDENT

MONROVIA, LIBERIA
September 12, 1958

Dear Rev. Guenter:

I acknowledge receipt of your very kind letter of the 6th instant, forwarding me some of the pictures taken on our trip.

It certainly was nice on your part to have done me this special favor, and I want to assure you very sincerely that I appreciate it very highly. I also appreciate the generous offer made for similar services in the future when an occasion arises. I shall not fail to contact you then.

Many thanks for your kind sentiments expressed in respect to my role in State and church, and for the Christian literature sent, which I find interesting.

With kindest regards and best wishes,

Sincerely yours,

Rev. Abraham Guenter
Pilot of the Baptist Plane
Mid-Liberia Baptist Mission
MONROVIA

LIBERIA

Daughter Suzanne (born in Africa) with her caretaker friend Mary, who became a leper

Abe in a new Super Cub, 1965, at Lock Haven, Pennsylvania

*Left to right:
Dale Kronemeyer, Bobby Smith,
son Darrell with big pineapple, and son Wesley*

*1969 crash
after engine failure
(Maule Aircraft). Left to right:
Albert Ostrander, Mike Lyons and J. T. Lyons*

A little girl afflicted with worms. After treatment, she was healed and walked home, a three-day trek.

Wife Susie with a baby from a village

A gospel quartet from our Bible school.
Left to right: Enoch, Solomon, Jeff, Lesley

Dr. Allan E. Lewis and wife,
Ann, in the back of the Super Cub, Liberia

*All our family
except two grandchildren—
"The Guenter Tribe"*

*Wayne and Suzanne
Bertness
(our daughter and
son-in-law)
and family—
Crystal, Michael,
Angela and
Michelle—
singers and
evangelists
to children*

to feel it out for a landing. The village was filled with people who had come from miles around for market day. They were getting excited as I buzzed around, for most of them had never seen an airplane. Later the villagers told me that a woman who was washing her clothes by the river with her baby on her back when I came buzzing low toward her got so scared that she threw her baby into the water and herself on top of it.

As I flew overhead, Dr. Reiber was ready to operate on a Liberian. The patient was all cleaned up and lying on the operating table with the nurses standing around. When the doctor heard my airplane, he looked out the window, wondering what was happening, for he knew Zorzor had no landing field.

On my fourth approach for a landing, I came slipping over the trees, gliding down to the grass. As I straightened out, the wheels kissed the ground. Applying brakes, I came to a gentle stop, close to the great crowd that had gathered on the edge of the compound. When I opened the cockpit and jumped out, the crowd erupted into a great chorus of shouting and cheers. They had not expected a man to appear out of the "iron bird."

As I approached the crowd, I saw the doctor come pushing through the crowd toward me, all out of breath. "Abe, did you have a forced landing?" he asked.

"No," I replied. "I came to see you, Doc. We need your help for a very sick missionary." We talked awhile; then he turned to the nurse.

"Mary, what do you suppose happened to the patient we left on the operating table?" She didn't know either, but when they looked behind them, there he was, standing in his white gown. He was not about to be left out of all the excitement! The village people were so excited about the airplane that the next day they all went out to the airfield that they had begun to build. They meant to finish it "just now," as they say over there!

The doctor welcomed me warmly, so I spent the night there. I had met him when he first arrived in Liberia and we all had slept in the army barracks that first night. I enjoyed his company and asked him, "Doc, what brings you out here?"

"The Lord has saved my soul," he answered, "and He is so good to me, I wanted to do something hard for Him." I liked his answer. We became good friends that night. Things were indeed hard for him out there in the deep jungle with no electricity, transportation or refrigeration except for the extremely inefficient "icy ball" (a cooling device) that had to be heated daily in a charcoal fire. Sometimes he had to operate by flashlight, and even medicines were hard to get.

I flew back the next day and brought Ellie Munter so the kind doctor could take care of her. He treated her and freed her from her fear of cancer. She served in Liberia for 30 years, teaching missionaries' kids, running the native school and doing medical work. She was our coworker at Zondo most of our time there. What a missionary!

We did not have another place to take our sick, so many times that little plane would plow its way through the clouds, wind and rain all the way to Zorzor. For instance, Pastor Gbayu's son Joseph once became deathly ill, and though the clouds and steam from the jungle together with the heavy rain made visibility zero, I felt I must try to save his life. Another student (a chief's son), Abba, begged to go along to help him en route.

We laid Joseph on the stretcher, eased him into the plane and, with Abba sitting beside him, I taxied to the end of the runway. We committed ourselves to the Lord in prayer. Then I pushed the throttle all the way in, the engine roared, and we leaped into the pouring rain, hopping from tree to tree. By this time I had learned the art of jungle hopping. The closer one kept to the trees, the farther he could see. (Similarly, the more you humble yourself before the Lord, the more you can see of God too!) Then it looked as if we were going to lose Joseph.

"Maybe we should turn back," Abba suggested fearfully. But I decided to plow on. Finally after an hour, we found Zorzor, landed and placed Joseph into the capable hands of my doctor friend. Joseph lived to become a great leader and a blessing to many.

A Super Cub Arrives
(Super Cub to the Rescue!?)

By 1950 we had gone home for furlough and brought back our first Super Cub with flaps. We could not believe all that the new airplane could do, for it had almost twice the horsepower, was a little roomier and had two big gas tanks and flaps. What a workhorse! I decided we needed more seats in it, so I fixed an additional seat between the front and back seats and discovered that two small people could fit into the backseat. Then I put a small seat into the baggage compartment and belts on the extra seats so we could easily carry five people.

Shortly after the new plane's arrival, a Pan American Clipper crashed in heavy rain. It flew right into the side of a hill, and forty-three bodies scattered everywhere. One boy's head was caught right in the crotch of a tree, and he was hanging there about 20 feet up in the air. What a tragedy!

A DC3 airplane from Roberts Airport came over our place and dropped a message for me: "Abe, will you please come and help in rescue work?" I kissed Susie good-bye.

"When will you be back?" she asked.

"Who knows?" I replied honestly and took off. A small landing field was located one hour's walk from the crash sight. My plane was the only one that could land on this small strip; therefore, I made many flights for the investigation crew, newsmen and government officials.

One flight was unusual. I had to transport the chief over all Pan Am personnel of Europe, Asia and Africa; Pan Am's senior lawyer and Pan Am's chief mechanic.

"This is a Super Cub," I said, rather proud of our new plane, "so you will all fit inside it. Who will take the baggage compartment?" The chief of personnel, having been a great commercial pilot himself for many years, was a good sport and volunteered. He folded his six-foot frame into the back. The lawyer took the rear seat, and the chief mechanic got on the jump seat. After flipping the prop, I climbed into the pilot's seat and took off. As we were cruising along, I hollered back to them, "If you guys get sick back there, let me know; I have a bag for you."

"What other services does your airline provide?" the chief in the back wanted to know, chuckling.

It was a beautiful sunny day, with a few clouds hanging on the hills. When we came to a ridge of small mountains, I noticed they were covered with clouds too, but I could see a small hole between two peaks. I knew that a wide open valley lay on the other side, so I decided to have some fun with my passengers. I aimed the plane's nose for the small hole, which my passengers could not see. When things got a bit dark in the clouds, the chief in the baggage compartment hollered, "Abe, what are you doing?" But when in a moment we shot down into the clear valley, he said, "Great! I'm right with you!"

To walk the jungle trail was a great experience for them, but to see the tragedy was a great shock. In the afternoon I flew them back to Roberts Airport, and when they had all extricated themselves from my Super Cub, the big chief kicked the tire and turned to me. "Abe," he declared, "that is quite a machine! I never had any use for the Cubs that always got in my way when I was landing the big ones, but I have changed my mind completely today. Thank you very much for a great day!"

I flew many more flights before the funeral. What a sad time. The bodies of those forty-three passengers had to be rushed down from the hills and buried quickly. The officials had the natives dig two big holes, build two large boxes, lay all the bodies into them and nail them shut, but the bodies began to swell and the boxes pushed apart. The funeral service was short. Before long they covered the sorrowful sight with a few feet of earth. A man came from Europe, wanting to claim the bodies of his dear wife and child. He was beside himself with grief, and when the Pan Am official told him it would be impossible to take their bodies, he pulled out a revolver. With tears in his eyes, he blurted out, "Don't tell me that!" The officials were able to calm him down and help him to understand that they really could not give him the bodies of his loved ones. Then they put a lovely marker on the grave site. It is still there today.

The God Mountain!!

About 60 air miles east of Monrovia was a mountain that had a strange look to it from the north side, sort of like a face. In the mornings when the fog rose from the mountain, it looked as if it were steaming or smoking as though it had a big fire inside. The people worshiped this mountain and said that no airplane could ever fly over it, for on top of the mountain was a great lake that was guarded by a big fish. If any airplane should try to fly over it, the fish would spew a great flood of water at it and blow the airplane out of the sky.

Many times I had flown by this mountain, and I did not know all this superstition. Then missionaries began to reach out to these benighted people. They then encouraged the people to build an airfield, and the chief really got excited, for an airstrip would put his village on the map. I began to notice the activity below as I flew over. From way up there it looked as if a bunch of ants were clearing a narrow strip in the jungle. I kept watching as the strip grew longer and longer until one day the missionaries asked me to drop in.

When I arrived and circled to land, I could see the native people come running from their farms and villages. They all wanted to see the iron bird drop from the sky onto the landing field they had worked so hard to build.

When I touched down smoothly and rolled to a stop in front of the big crowd of mostly naked people, they shouted and danced and warmly welcomed me.

After a while the missionary told me the story of the 'god mountain,' and I became excited. "Let's go and see for ourselves; jump in!" I said. The people asked us where we were going, and we told them, "We want to see the big fish up there."

They pleaded, "Oh please! We don't want you to die today. Please, please don't go!"

Nevertheless we took off, and the people held their breath as we climbed steadily toward their god. They were sure they would never see us again. When we disappeared out of sight on the other side of the mountain, they said, "We told them not to do that." They were sure we had died, but we were only circling, looking for any possible water. We covered the whole mountain and saw no lake and, of course, no fish. As we came gliding down and lined up with the airstrip, we rolled to a stop right in front of them. They exclaimed, "You mean you did not die?"

I replied, "No, someone told you a big fish story; there is no lake up there and no fish. Why don't you rather worship the great God of Heaven and earth Who made this mountain and all things you see?"

The Bible says, "The times of this ignorance God winked at; but now commandeth all men every where to repent: Because he hath appointed a day, in the which he will judge the world in righteousness by that man [Jesus] whom he hath ordained" (Acts 17:30, 31).

The airplane had done it again, helping them to turn from darkness to light and from the power of Satan unto God.

A "Devil Woman" Saved!!

Nikpo was short and slight, but she was powerful. She was the head of the Women's Zo (the strong native secret society), demon-powered and in control of the women. She lived in Nijiwen.

For Nikpo to become a Christian would mean laying aside all that power and prestige and burning her witchcraft. She had made up her mind that she would never give her heart to Jesus.

One day, however, I came in for a landing on the path beside the church. This path had been widened enough for my wings to clear the bush. The landing strip was only 400 feet long, and a pilot really had to be on his toes to land there. Before this I used to walk three hours from the big Roberts Airport, but now I could land right beside the church.

When darkness fell, we lit the kerosene lanterns, and the people filled the church, listening eagerly to the Word of God. The local pastor, Charlie, could read and preach, but it was always special when "Teachah Gantah" came flying in.

As we enjoyed fellowship in the house of the Lord (a thatched mud house), Nikpo's curiosity was aroused. Nikpo came in the darkness and hid behind a palm tree. She wanted no one to see her listening to God's Word. But God's Word is powerful, and that night, as the Word entered her ear, it also went into her mind and heart.

As we were singing the last hymn, she backed off into the darkness and slipped into her little hut for the night. She said to herself, "God, eternal life, a city of gold, no pain, hunger or death: that is beautiful, but it can never be for me, for I am the big Zo. I must forget about all that." She lay down on her grass mat on the floor and tried to forget about it all and go to sleep, but sleep escaped her. She rolled over on her other side, but still the Spirit of God spoke to her.

"He that believeth not shall be damned. Do you want to go to everlasting fire?" She rolled over again, but still sleep eluded her. The conviction of the Holy Spirit was heavy upon her.

She tossed and turned until about midnight then finally got up, opened the door and, slipping through the darkness, went to the pastor's window. She stood there for a while and finally said, "Bock, bock." (Liberians don't knock on doors; they say "bock, bock.") She waited, but hearing no stirring within, she spoke a little louder. "BOCK, BOCK." Pastor Charlie stirred and called out,

"Who's that?"

"That's me," she said in a guarded voice. (Liberians know each other in the dark by their voices.)

"You!" he exclaimed. "Why do you come to my window in the night like this?"

"Pastor, I listened to God's words tonight from behind the palm tree, and I have come to believe."

"Good," he said. "Go bring all your witchcraft; then we will pray together for you to be saved."

"Oh, no!" she protested. "You know I can never do that."

"Then you are not ready to believe and follow Jesus. Go back to your hut," he replied.

With slow steps, drooping shoulders and a heavy heart, Nikpo slowly retraced her steps and lay down again to sleep. But the Holy Spirit did not give up. The conviction continued in her heart, and after a few hours she returned to the pastor's window. "Bock, bock," she said. Pastor Charlie stirred and raised himself on his elbow.

"Who's that?"

"That's me again. I really want to follow Jesus."

"Did you bring the witchcraft?" he asked.

"Pastor, it belongs to my people, and the Devil just won't let me. I can't," she wailed.

"Yes, you can; Jesus will help you. Go back," he said firmly.

She turned around, and as she walked to her hut, she prayed. "Oh, Jesus, will You help me, please?"

As she entered her hut, she grabbed the box full of idols and witchcraft and quickly retraced her steps. At the window she whispered excitedly, "Pastor, I did it, I did it! Now will you show me the Jesus road?" There in the darkness, the Devil woman was led to Jesus, the Light of the World, and was gloriously saved! Born again! Praise God! Instead of serving the Devil, she became the choir leader in the church. She would walk many miles to conferences, giving her testimony and singing for Jesus. Her black face just glowed with the glory of God. ". . . I am not ashamed of the gospel of Christ: for it is the power of God unto salvation to every one that believeth . . ." (Rom. 1:16).

I Baptized Lutherans by Immersion

Mr. Stelling, a single Lutheran missionary, asked me to fly him to Zorzor one sunny day with just a few fluffy clouds floating around. As we approached one of these clouds, I asked him, "Stelling, have you ever been baptized by immersion?"

"No," he replied.

"In that case," I teased him, "I'm going to do it for you right now," and we entered into one of those lovely soft billowy clouds. When we came out the other side, I asked him, "What do you say now?"

"Thank you!" he answered.

Some days later my friend, Dr. Reiber, came up the road and asked for a flight to Zorzor too. We piled his gear and baggage into the Super Cub and took off. Again it was a lovely day with those same soft fluffy clouds floating here and there. I said to him, "Doc, did you know that I baptized your missionary, Stelling, by immersion the other day?"

"No," he replied, "I guess that makes him a little better than the rest of us."

"Yes, and I am going to baptize you right now too," as we flew straight into a cloud. It got a bit dark. Then as we popped out the other side, he had become a Baptist! The incident reminded me of 1 Corinthians 10:1 and 2: "Our fathers . . . were all baptized unto Moses in the cloud. . . ."

Special Flights

Many people asked me to make special flights, like the time the Christian radio station ELWA first began. Bill Watkins had just come to look things over.

"Abe," he requested, "please take me up and let me look things over from above for the best location to set up the radio station." We flew around for a while. Then he spotted a nice place near the hill and on the beach, which he ultimately chose for their site. The station grew and became a mighty voice for the gospel.

When Uniroyal Rubber was planning to start a plantation in Liberia, various officials asked me to fly them around. We flew all over central Liberia, after which they established their plantation right next to us in Bassa County. Because of this relationship, the company granted us many favors through the years.

The LAMCO Iron Ore Company needed a railroad. Their spokesmen came to me. "Abe, can you fly our expert for railroad building along this route I have marked on the map, just 50 feet above the treetops?"

"Sure," I replied, "that's my territory." As a result of the man's survey, LAMCO changed their plans and saved millions of dollars.

Several lumber companies had me fly their tree specialists to evaluate the forests. In half an hour I saved them months of time. Roads were built as a result, and the country opened up. This development also opened new doors for the gospel.

When R. G. LeTourneau came to Liberia in 1953, we made a number of survey flights for him. He picked a spot on the beach at Baffu Bay. When I flew him into the place, we were flying low along the beach. The jungle there was intertwined and twisted together like a mat.

"Pretty wild-looking place, huh?" I remarked.

"Well," he said, "it is about time somebody tamed it a bit."

I made twenty-seven flights for him, carrying in his team plus many government officials. Even the Speaker of the House of Representatives came. Since he was a small man, I decided to put him into the baggage compartment. All the men were good sports and were willing to be squeezed into the Super Cub; the flights were only a short seven minutes. One of the officials brought along a case of liquor. I said politely, "This is a mission plane, and I am afraid that God would not bless us if I fly that stuff. We might crash, and you don't want that, do you?"

"No," he said, so we left the liquor behind.

We spent the night in tents, sleeping on camp cots, waiting for the morning when LeTourneau's ship would beach nearby. We had plenty of time to talk and witness. When I went to inspect the plane the next morning, I found bush cow and even elephant tracks all around the plane. I thanked the Lord for keeping the animals from demolishing my plane.

Soon we could see the ship coming in the distance, so we all walked the ten minutes to where it was to beach. While we waited there, sitting on the sand, the same gentleman who had had the liquor the day before came and sat down in the sand beside me and said, "You do me bad yesterday."

"Now what bad thing did I do?" I asked. "Did I not fly you safely in here?"

"Oh yes, you did," he admitted, "but you know that . . ." and pretending he had a bottle in his hand, held it toward his mouth and tilted his head back.

"Oh, *that!*" I said. "Well, you would not really expect a mission airplane to fly liquor, would you?"

"No, I guess not," he replied.

Then the small ship plowed right into the beach. It was unbelievable to see all the heavy machinery, equipment and even an airplane coming out of the belly of that small ship. It was a big day for Liberia, and the government officials all seemed ecstatic as we flew them back out again.

The government compound along the coast tried to construct an airfield, but it had chosen the wrong place. With the Super Cub, I was able to squeeze into the 300-foot clearing. The officials were excited and thankful! I preached the Word of God first and then talked them into building the airfield on a more suitable site. That week the Monrovia newspaper came out with a full story about my landing and the great help I had given the officials.

In those early days President Tubman asked me to make a flight for him to Tchein, a last outpost by the back border of Liberia. I couldn't make the flight due to some trouble I was having with my engine. While waiting for parts to come from the United States, I stayed with my friend, Herb Congo, a WEC missionary. On Sunday he said, "Abe, let's go to the Methodist church today; the President is going to be there."

"OK," I agreed, so we went.

After the service, we saw President Tubman go out and stand on the corner, waiting for his wife. I approached him and said, "Sir, I am pilot Guenter. You asked me to make a flight to Tchein, and I am so sorry I was unable to do that for you, due to engine trouble."

"Isn't that just like God," he said. "Just when we need Him most, then He is gone, or at least it seems like that." My friend Herb backed up and took a picture of the two of us. Later I was involved in flying Vice President Tolbert. I took his picture on that occasion and gave it to him, which initiated a friendship with him too.

A Pilot's Most Thrilling Experience

It was conference time, and I was flying in my last passenger, Dale Kronemeyer. The day was hot and windy, a bad day for flying. The conditions caused the plane to bounce all over the sky. Dale was sitting beside me in the Cub when I noticed him beginning to squirm. His ears and neck began to turn pale; I knew trouble was on the way. Finally I took off my brand-new helmet and handed it to him. "Dale, if you have to use it, go ahead." Soon he did, and kept on until the liquid ran out of the little holes. "You had better give it to me now," I suggested. I planned to empty it out the window. When I got the hat halfway out the window, the wind caught it just right and blew the contents back into my face. I saw nothing for a while (talk about blind flying!), but after wiping my eyes, I was able to see enough to land safely.

Lud Zerbe had a similar experience. Virginia Lillard was given to airsickness. One day Lud was flying her, and it was one of those rough days when the plane bounces all over the sky. Virginia happened to be sitting on the jump seat between the two seats of the Super Cub. Lud's shirt was wide open at the neck as he bent forward, cruising along. All of a sudden she got the urge, and it all spouted down his neck! What a shocking experience! But Lud never lost control, and they landed safely. The first thing he looked for, however, was a bath and a clean shirt! I don't blame him.

Sometime later, this same missionary became seriously ill, and we had to rush her home. A Pan Am flight for New York was leaving at 5:00 A.M., so we flew to Roberts Airport and put her on that early flight. As the big clipper took off, I noticed that the sky was clear that particular morning at dawn, so we took off for Monrovia. Coming along the beach toward ELWA radio station, by then in operation, I decided to drop down onto the road. I taxied the plane right in front of the house of my friend Bill Thompson. The right wing ended up under his overhanging roof. He looked out with surprise written all over his face, and I hollered, "How are the pancakes coming?" We had a short but pleasant surprise visit with him and his family and then left for Monrovia. Eventually we went home to Zondo.

Snakes and Ants

W alt and Ruth Kronemeyer's son, Dale, was a real jungle boy and learned all the tricks the native boys knew. I flew Trader Horn in there one day, and he talked Dale into catching a lot of snakes for him. One day Dale called me on the radio.

"Uncle Abe, when you fly into Monrovia tomorrow, would you swing around here and pick up me and my snakes? I have a good bunch now for Trader Horn."

"OK, Dale," I said. "You can look for me first thing in the

morning." The next morning he called back.

"Uncle Abe, the driver ants got into the cages last night and ate up all my snakes; all that is left is skeletons."

The Baby Is White!

Floyd and Francis Holmes, great missionaries, worked with the Kronemeyers deep in the jungles beyond Tappi near the Ivory Coast border. They saw a great turning to the Lord among the Krahn tribe; people who had been far from God were brought nigh, praise God!

Around the time that Dale Kronemeyer was collecting snakes, Francis Holmes needed to go to the hospital for the birth of her new baby. The native people were excited about that. When I finally brought her back, they were all eyes. When they saw the baby, they gasped in surprise. "Oh! The baby is white!" they exclaimed. They expected it would be born black since it was born in black man's country.

When our daughter Suzanne was about to be born, we decided to stay on the station and have Carolyn Hovingh come for the delivery because she was a good midwife. However, I had asked the doctor at the coast to keep his bag packed. I planned to buzz his house and pick him up in case of an emergency. But everything went just fine, and we were thrilled with a daughter. She has been special ever since. All our Zondo people were excited, for they, too, expected her to be born black.

Lightning Strikes the Plane

Sometime later I returned to Nijiwen for another Sunday. Sunday afternoon was like a Bible school. David Summerville was the pastor's helper. His notebook usually had about 25 questions he would ask me about the Bible, and others put in their questions too. Later he became the pastor for the big Calvary Baptist Church in Monrovia.

After the evening service we all went to bed, and a big storm blew up. Lightning struck all over, and the wind blew fiercely. I prayed that the ropes with which I had tied the plane down would hold. Suddenly a great bolt of lightning flashed through the sky and struck nearby, which stunned us all. The children on the floor cried with pain, and a woman down the hill was paralyzed for three hours from the shock.

The lightning struck a tall papaya tree and burned it to a frazzle. The electric current followed the water in the gutter alongside the church. My airplane wings were right in line with it and, as it shot toward the landing gear, it clipped the grass, making it look as though it had been cut by a lawn mower. The current went all through the plane, part of it shooting out the other wheel, blowing off the cover and then running down the hill, cutting the grass. Part of the current went into the tail of the plane and to the ground, digging a trench and plowing its way into the ditch.

In the morning we gathered for prayer in the church and thanked God for keeping us. People in Liberia believe that those who give themselves to Satan can go in the spirit, roam in the sky and shoot lightning down on their enemies. One man said, "Somebody tried to shoot our church, but he missed."

I carefully examined the airplane for damage. When I started it up, it ran nicely. In flight, I noticed that my compass was off 40 percent in some directions. The whole plane had been magnetized, so I made note of my new compass headings. As I continued to fly, my compass slowly returned to normal, but it took four months!

Teachah Gantah, Our Missy Is Dying!

A native boy came running to my house, all out of breath, with a letter in his hand. He had sped through the jungles for 18 miles to bring me the sad news that his tribe's missionary was dying. I read the letter hurriedly, said good-bye to Susie and ran toward the airplane. I always kept it ready to go, so it did not take long to push it out of the hangar, flip the prop and get underway. In seven minutes we landed at Gay Peter. We walked up the hill, and I followed the lad into Miss Kay Tullis's bedroom. What a sight! Her fever was so intense that the whole bed shook from her trembling.

No one except schoolboys was around to help me carry her. They brought a hammock. I was glad I was strong and not small. I used to think a missionary pilot ought to be a small man so he could carry more payload, but I have changed my mind about that! Miss Kay weighed around 160 pounds, and all alone I had to lift her into the hammock, then into the plane.

When I started the engine and closed the door, Miss Kay pleaded, "Please close the window too; I am so cold." It was 90 degrees, but for good measure I pulled on the heater too. We took off, and all the way to Monrovia I wiped my perspiration.

At that time the city had no airfield, but the people had dredged the new harbor and spread a lot of clean glistening sand along the shore, which made a perfect place for us to touch down. I lined up for an approach, came in for a nice smooth landing and rolled to a stop close to the road. It was a holiday, and the traffic was lighter than usual. But then I noticed a shiny black limousine come rolling along from the harbor with an American flag fluttering on the fender. I knew it was the American ambassador, so I flagged him down. As he opened the window, I saluted him.

"Sir, I just landed here with this very sick missionary. Would you be so kind as to give us a lift into the city?"

"Bring her," he said without hesitation. All by myself I had to lift her out, carry her to the limousine and slide her into the backseat. When we got into the city, I had to carry her up three flights of stairs at the mission house. Was I bushed!! The doctor found she had three tropical fevers, each one bad enough to kill her, but she lived and continued serving the Lord.

On another day I was asked to fly a German missionary lady to the coast, for she was sure she was dying of cancer. She wept during the entire two-hour flight. I felt so sorry for her, but a few weeks later I had the joy of flying her back to her station, all smiles. She did not have cancer after all.

Some time later I flew back to Zorzor for another medical emergency. One of the Lutheran nurses there was in critical condition. The other missionaries prepared her for evacuation and brought her to the plane in a stretcher. After we were airborne, I turned around and spoke with her, but she did not respond. Her hair blew all over her face, but she never moved. When I arrived at Suakoko, we unloaded her into a camp bed and carried her, unconscious, into a pretty blue room in the home of a Baptist missionary there. After her head had been down for a while, she began to stir, and as she looked around and saw the blue walls, she determined she was in Heaven. But where were her Lutheran friends? All she could see were Baptists! Soon, however, when the Lutheran missionaries arrived in their station wagon to pick her up, she began to realize she was not in Heaven after all!

Bugs Bug Us!

I hate bedbugs!

I often flew over a particular town, and the people there always waved to me. One day two men and I walked into the jungle, headed for the town to evangelize it. When we walked into the place, the people were excited to see the man who always flew over their village, and they welcomed me warmly. They cooked a nice dinner for me, and everybody wanted to hear the words of God. It was a good time.

Then they gave me their best bed. It was too short for me, however, and the poles under the grass mattress cracked when I laid down on it. But with care I was able to straighten out under my mosquito net. Because I was exhausted, I went to sleep almost immediately. After a few hours, I woke up with terrible itching and what seemed like an army of insects crawling over me. I flicked on my flashlight and, sure enough, I was covered by bedbugs. They were all over my net too. There were big ones, middle-sized ones and tiny ones. When I mashed them they stank. What a night I had! Even though I killed most of the first ones, others came to join them as though they were coming to their funeral!! They crawled all through my hair and clothing, and I felt "crawly" all day until I got home and took a hot bath with lots of soap.

Susie had a similar experience with bedbugs. In the morning, her guide and helper, a civilized man, apologized, "Oh Missy, we are sorry we forgot to check your bed, but they don't bother us. They must have come to welcome you as their stranger [guest]!"

Another critter that really bugged us at Zondo was the jigger. Jiggers are little fellows, so small that you can just barely see them. They usually like to jump on your toe, find the crack by your nail and burrow in. Once they are into your skin, the toe starts itching terribly. Then after a while it feels OK again, but it is not. Next they lay about a thousand eggs, and the sac grows into the size of a small pea until it is "ripe." Then the sack bursts open, and the baby jiggers spread into the dust or into your shoe and start the process all over again. If people don't dig out the jiggers, the whole bottom of the foot will get covered with these "nests."

We had a chimpanzee that the native boys liked to tease. When they came over to see him, they would unintentionally spread jigger babies from their feet, and the jiggers would then burrow into the chimp's feet and make their nests. We always had a mess on our hands trying to dig them out.

At one place where I preached, the chief used to listen to the Word, but then he started to drink and did many wicked things. One day, in his drunken state he beat and cursed his own mother. The next morning, when he was sober, I rebuked him for it and told him Judgment Day is coming. "Yes, I did bad," he conceded.

One day a jigger got into his toe. He had it dug out, but it did not feel good. The paramount chief called him to come for a big meeting, a two-days' journey away. He did not want to go because his foot hurt him so much. But the people said, "When the big chief calls you, you must go," so he started out. After the first day, his foot swelled up, and he did not want to go on. Still the people said, "Let us try to go; we will help you." He went on, but his foot kept on swelling until it looked like a balloon. Blood poisoning had set in, and he died. When I heard of his death, I told the people, "God uses big things and little things to do His work. 'Be sure your sin will find you out' " (Num. 32:23).

Corbett Saved

Gene Corbett and his family came to Liberia in 1950. He was a tall, thin, former Navy man. His wife Carol was short, plump and cheerful. She was also full of music and was a really good singer. They settled in at Yila with the Dick Millers. Soon the people loved them. One day when I flew in with the mail and supplies, I discovered Gene was rather sick. I did not think his illness was too serious, for we all got sick some time or other in that "white man's grave" as Africa was called.

A few days passed, and I began to have an uneasy feeling. We still had no radio contact, but God moved on my heart to direct me to go and see what was wrong. On landing at the supply base, Suakoko, I met Gene and the family, for the missionaries had carried him out of Yila and were wondering how they could rush him and the family home.

That night no one slept much. Karl Luyben stayed with Gene in the Rahilly house, seeing to it that he took the medicine the doctor at the Ganta hospital had prescribed. But Gene, out of his mind from the cerebral malaria that had attacked him, did strange things. As the first rooster crowed in the morning he remarked, "Karl, you hear that rooster crowing? That is the voice of God telling me, 'Don't take any more medicine.' "

"No, it's not," Karl said, and with that, he ran out the door, chasing that rooster with a big washtub in hand. Finally he cornered him right under my window in the big house and slammed the tub down on him. I raised myself on my elbow and looked out the window.

"Karl, what on earth are you doing chasing after a rooster at four o'clock in the morning?" He quietly told me what Gene had said. When he returned to Gene, there was, of course, no rooster crowing anymore, so he was able to persuade Gene to take his medicine.

By daybreak we had made our plans. Gene, Karl, Catherine Mellish (a nurse) and I would fly down to Monrovia, and the rest would go overland 120 miles by road. I decided to detour to Roberts Airport and try to make reservations for five to fly home that night. When I approached the Pan Am agent and asked for five reservations for that night, he was incredulous. "Abe, this is the last flight before Christmas, and there is never an empty seat. No way!"

"Anyway, we are coming to wait on standby for tonight's flight," I persisted.

"You can come," he conceded, "but I hold out no hopes for you."

We got ready to fly to Monrovia to check Gene and his family out of the country with the proper officials. Karl took the baggage compartment again; we put Gene in the backseat; Catherine sat on the jumpseat to hold Gene down; and I took the pilot's seat. As we taxied for take-off, I decided to swing by where the Canadian Aerial Photographic team was. Now get this picture! Here we were, four large people jammed into a Super Cub with the engine idling. I waved for one of the fellows to come over, and as he was coming, I hollered, "Are you guys going home for Christmas?" (thinking this might be a way to get Gene home).

"No, Abe," he answered. "We won't be going home 'till March." Then Gene piped up from his cramped, barely visible position.

"Never mind, Mack. We are going home in our own plane." The guy's mouth dropped open, and I knew strange thoughts were going through his mind, so I quickly shut the door and took off for Monrovia.

On the way, Gene shouted at me from behind Catherine, "Abe, I know God is going to give us a new plane, and I know it's going to be a Silvaire." I just agreed with him. Just then a Liberian Airways DC3 was coming by on our right, and he shouted again, "There it is, Abe. Follow him!"

"Let's go to Monrovia first, Gene," I said, and he didn't protest.

When the whole party, Catherine Mellish, Eleanor Brittain and the Corbett family had been checked out of the country, we all went to Roberts Airport to wait on standby. At 10:00 P.M. I went over to operations to see if space might be available on the midnight flight. As soon as the agent saw me, he became excited. "Aren't you going to bring the baggage?" he asked.

"You mean you have room for all?"

"Abe, this is strange," he mused, "but five people failed to show up at Johannesburg, so we can take them all."

"Praise the Lord!" I shouted while I ran down to the barracks, collected the baggage and rushed our party over.

One hitch though: Pan Am would not take any seriously ill passengers unless they had a doctor's written guarantee that they would not cause any trouble on the flight. Because Catherine was a great nurse and the Firestone doctor had full confidence in her, he wrote out a guarantee for her. Then, just before the flight, Catherine gave Gene a sedative. Karl picked him up in his arms and carried him on board and, as God would have it, Gene and Catherine were able to sit right next to the bathroom.

The Pan Am Clipper winged them over the great Atlantic Ocean, and the next day Gene was put into the hands of a malaria specialist in New York City. He hung in the balance for a week, but then he began to return to his senses and eventually to good health. The doctor said, "If he had been six hours later in getting here, he would never have made it." Another "score" for the Super Cub, another life saved. Praise God!

Big Spider, Don't Bite Me

In Liberia, we missionaries enjoyed the *Reader's Digest*. On my many flights when I had nothing much to do except listen to the drone of the airplane or enjoy the scenery, I either memorized Scripture or read the *Reader's Digest*.

On lovely days when the birds had gone north for the summer and the engine ran smoothly, I would relax and pull down my *Digest* from the dash. With one eye on the instruments, one on my flight path and another on the *Digest,* I would gain much valuable information and pleasure.

On one of those sunny, clear days, I was ready to take off from Zondo station in the Super Cub with two people in the backseat and a bunch of bananas in the baggage compartment. As the engine idled at the end of the field, we prayed and then poured the power to the 150 horses.

We leaped into the air, and I was just entering into a left turn when I felt something come over the bare skin of my right leg between my sock and my pant leg. I took a quick squint down to see what it was, and I nearly froze at the controls. A big hairy tarantula with big beady eyes stood on my knee cap, looking me over.

As I leveled off, I changed from right hand to left on the control stick to be farther from him. Then, with my right hand free, I looked around frantically for something to swat him with. He was holding his position as I spotted my new *Reader's Digest* by the windshield. I reached for it slowly, all the while hoping that my two native passengers would not see him. Would they jump out if they did? I grabbed the book firmly and slowly brought it into position to swat the spider. He now moved into a perfect position on the wall just beside me, so with one swift swing I brought the book down on him—WHAM! The juice and legs went flying, but we were saved—by the *Reader's Digest!* I decided to write the story and send it to the *Digest.* In turn, they sent me a check.

It Is Leprosy!

Mary was an eight-year-old native girl who began to help take care of our new baby, Suzanne. She taught Suzanne the Bassa language, carried her on her back and was a great help to my wife, Susie, who had many responsibilities in the mission schools teaching our own boys and in helping with the medical work. Then in 1955 we went on furlough. When we returned, we were asked to work at Suakoko. Mary came with us and continued capably helping with Suzanne.

One day Mary cried, "Missy, I don't know what to do! The skin on my back is on fire and itches too much—o. What is the matter?" As God would have it, a lady specialist in leprosy had joined us for lunch that day.

"Let me check her out," she suggested. With a chicken feather she went all over Mary's back, touching lightly here and there and asking Mary when she felt the feather. Then came the shocker. She said to Susie, "There are two spots on her back that have no feeling; she has leprosy."

"Oh no!" we both cried. "She has carried Suzanne on that infected back now for several years. Do you think our little girl might have it too?"

"We won't know for perhaps five more years," she said sympathetically. Could we wait that long? Yes, we could. We cast our burden on the Lord, He sustained us, and Suzanne did not contract leprosy. Praise God!

I flew Mary to the Yila Leprosy Colony, and one of the native Christian women in the colony took her in and became her new mother. Nurse Carolyn Hovingh immediately began to treat her, and so her new way of life began. Living with so many suffering people hit Mary hard. She even talked of suicide, but we encouraged her to keep trusting the Lord and to take her medicine faithfully. In two years she began running negative skin tests, and then finally Carolyn was able to give her the "Clean Certificate." It was a happy day when I flew her back home.

In that leper colony lived a small leper man with unusually short legs. Everybody called him "Ugly." One day he asked Carolyn, "Missy, can I work for you?"

"Well, would you be willing to clean the terrible ulcers on these leprosy patients?" she asked.

"Yes, Missy," he answered. So day after day he did that stinky, messy work. I watched him one day and, believe me, his job was awful. Ugly was faithful in coming to the services and listening attentively to God's Word. One day he opened his heart to the Lord and was gloriously saved.

"What shall we call him now?" Carolyn asked. "He has to have a new name." (It was the custom to change a person's name when he became a Christian.)

"Let's call him 'Beautiful,' " someone suggested. So that became his new name, and he became a beautiful witness for the Lord Jesus from then on.

My Engine Quit

As I was landing at Krahn one day, a goat came out of the jungle to my right. I was sitting on the left side in my new Tri-Pacer airplane and could not see him. He met the plane in the middle of the runway and knocked the nose wheel out from under it. The nose went down; the propeller chewed up the ground; and the plane almost flipped over. Fortunately, the nose cone flattened, and the plane skidded to a stop on it.

"What happened?" I wondered as I jumped out. A crowd had gathered, as usual. The people pointed to the back of the plane. There I saw the goat with his feet in the air, kicking his last.

The damage to the plane was extensive: a bent prop, a damaged crankshaft and a demolished nose wheel. We were laid up quite some time, waiting for parts from home. Finally they arrived, and the big job of repairing began.

We opened the engine to replace the crankshaft. During the reassembly in an open shed, I tried to be careful, but a few grains of sand managed to get in. After test-running the plane on the ground for some time, I finally took it up for a while. Everything was working well, so, taking Susie and Suzanne, I headed for Yila.

In 30 minutes we landed there safely, had a little visit and took off for Suakoko to arrive in time for Sunday services. The engine had good power. Soon we were airborne, but as I banked to the right, I lost all power. We started going down fast. Susie had Suzanne on her lap, and she quickly tightened the seat belt while we both cried out to God. Yet we were not scared because we were too busy for that. The missionaries on the station heard the engine cut out, and they cried out to the Lord too. Just before we plunged into the jungle, we regained full power suddenly. I whipped the plane around and headed back. Then it cut out again, but I had enough altitude to make a sharp left and to dive in for a safe landing.

I did my trouble-shooting and found one of my intake valves holding open. I took out the hydraulic tappets and found one sticking because of one or two grains of sand. After a careful cleaning job and reassembly, I took the Tri-Pacer back into the air. I flew around for a while, then came down, loaded the family in and continued home, praising the Lord that His hand was still upon us.

Guts in My Soup!

When we moved to Suakoko in 1956, we had to learn a new tribal language. I studied hard and thought I was getting along quite well. David (my teacher) and I went out preaching one Saturday. When we arrived on foot in the village, which was far removed from the road, the people joyously greeted us. They welcomed me with the gift of a chicken, which they put into my hands. Then custom dictated that I return it to them to cook for me. I spoke the new language, using it as much as possible. David said I was doing well.

When the villagers had the feathers plucked off, they opened up the abdomen and gave the "guts" to the boys, who then strung them out on a big log, chopping them into pieces with a machete.

"Are you boys going to have a nice dinner?" I thought I asked. They looked so embarrassed that I knew I must have put a wrong tone on one of the words. They thought I was accusing them of being so selfish as to take the best parts of the chicken for themselves. So they scooped up all the guts in their hands and dropped them into the pot where my chicken was already cooking. Oh no! I turned to David. "Please would you explain to the boys that I was not accusing them of being selfish. Tell them they are very welcome to the guts." As David spoke, the cook took my chicken out, washed it and gave the guts back to the boys. Then she cooked my chicken in clean water, and I had a great chicken dinner with rice.

God Spoke in My Spirit

One time after a conference had ended and I had flown all the folks home safely, I headed down toward the coast to pick up a radio for my upcoming flight to Nigeria. I was going to see my brother, a missionary there, whom I had not seen in 15 years. All went well until I was over the densest jungle in Liberia. Then I began to run into some rain, so I dropped down close to the trees for better visibility. All of a sudden I realized that the rain had closed in behind me and that I would have to go on through that weather to the coast. As I hopped from tree to tree with the rain pelting my windshield, the engine became rough. I began to get scared.

Then it seemed as though the Lord Jesus sat beside me in my new Tri-Pacer saying, "You aren't feeling so good, are you, Abe?" That was an understatement!

"No," I replied. Then He spoke again.

"If it should be My will for you to crash in this deep, dense jungle so that you would never be heard from again, would you agree? Would you be willing?" I began to think of Susie and the family at Zondo waiting to hear that familiar drone of my airplane and the cry of the native people, "See Bo!" They always did that as soon as they heard me coming in the distance. There would be none of that. And what would happen to my family? Yet I knew God's will is good, acceptable and perfect. Finally I answered, "Yes, Lord, I can trust You. No good thing will You withhold from them that walk uprightly. I am willing."

Then the engine smoothed out; the rain stopped pelting my windshield; and the clouds lifted enough for me to be able to see. But most of all, a great peace and joy flooded my soul. It was like the day that a missionary from Africa appealed for new volunteers. I joined about 20 other young people in that great auditorium in Saskatoon to surrender for missionary service wherever He should choose.

> Oh the peace my Savior gives,
> Peace I never knew before,
> And my way has brighter grown,
> Since I learned to trust Him more.
> *—Source Unknown*

Big Snake, Little Snake!

We were asked to help out at Suakoko in 1956. It had been such a discouraging place in so many ways, but with a great welcome from the Moores, Minnie and Doric Lane and Nadyne Ricks, we joined hands to do all we could to preach the gospel. Soon we began to see fruit for our labor.

Since we had a road there, I bought an old Jeep station wagon. Together with the Bible school men, we began to preach most evenings. We spread out into all the villages along the road and then walked out into the jungle, using loudspeakers, gospel records and Bible filmstrips, that "by all means he might save some." I had six records in the native language to play, so in one village I began to play them in the morning. When my arm got tired of operating the manual phonograph, I taught a young fellow to do it. The boys played the records all day. As a result we had a revival, with many souls saved. The people would walk to the mission seven miles for church. I would take them back five miles along the road; they still had to walk into the jungle two more miles. Then many others from far away began to come, and I had to haul them back, too, until it became an impossible task. But we rejoiced in all the blessings.

On Sunday evenings all of us went out along the road, each of us to a different village. Then I would pick up the whole team, and we would set up in our own big town with four loudspeakers, music and preaching with filmstrips. We filled every hut with the gospel at full volume. One day the people of a village four miles away said that they had heard us. On another night when things were going just great with a big crowd all around us, someone shouted, "Kali! Kali!" (Snake! Snake!) What a stampede! The people messed up the wires on the speakers and knocked over the screen in their hurry to evacuate, but no one got bitten.

Someone had a dream that Judgment Day was coming on a particular Monday. That Sunday night we had a huge crowd; everybody wanted to get saved. I asked them to kneel in the dust and pray out loud for mercy and salvation. It was a great night as they knelt and prayed, but we had to leave the results to the Lord.

One night as we were setting up in a village, I wondered how we could do anything, for the managers of the dance hall had just turned on their music machine at full volume, and one could hardly hear himself think. I went over to the hall and pleaded, "Mr. Moore, would you please turn the volume down a bit? We are trying to preach the gospel across the street." He immediately shouted to the boys.

"Turn the music off and go listen to the gospel!" Was I surprised! I wondered if that could ever happen in America.

In another village I was visiting the chief. Sitting on his piazza, I opened up my record player and began to play a few records for him in his own language. He crouched down over the machine and looked and looked! Then he asked curiously, "Where is the little man in the box that is talking to me in my own language?" He was so captivated by that little man in the box and what he was saying! One of the Christians saw his intense interest.

"Chief," he asked, "how is it that you are listening to the Word of God today when you never did before?"

"When the iron starts to speak the Word of God," he replied, "then you *have* to listen!"

On another night we had ministered to several villages. As we returned in a heavy downpour, I saw a log in the middle of the road. I had swung to the right to miss it, but I saw it move and realized it was a big snake. I slammed on the brake and backed up, trying to run over it. But I missed and saw it slither through the ditch with great speed. I heard a loud groan from the passengers in the bus. "Oh no, Teachah. You missed him!" The Liberians loved snake steak.

Around that same time we had a close encounter with another snake. Starting our days at 5:30 A.M., we were quite washed out by noon, so it was a good practice to rest a bit after lunch. It helped a person escape the worst of the day's heat too. We called it "siesta," or as we would say, "I go to 'see Esther'!" Just as we finished our siesta on one particular day, a native boy came up to Susie.

"Missy, I saw a very bad snake go under your screen door into your house." So with brooms and sticks in hand, we began to search, literally pulling the whole house apart, but found nothing. A little later a neighboring missionary's son, Phillip Ozinga, came to play with Suzanne and, seeing her tricycle near the door, he jumped on it to take a ride. There under the seat lay the snake, all coiled up. When he felt the pressure on the seat, he slithered down to the floor, looking for a way of escape. Suzanne was right in his way, but our house boy, Chauncey, grabbed her by the arm and swept her up and out of the way. Then Chauncey's machete came down on that little snake, and he was no more. We sighed with relief, praising God for protection again. The little green mamba was only fifteen inches long, but it could have killed Suzanne within five minutes.

Darrell's Crash at Wheaton

We missionaries suffer a great deal because of being separated from our kids.

One day we heard that our son Darrell had been hurt in an accident. He was living at Mid-Maples, a home for missionary kids. The Moneysmiths (the houseparents) would take all the kids to different churches to sing and testify. They always were a great blessing.

On the night of the accident, they were heading out again with three carloads. The VW bus in front was coming to a green light. They moved ahead, but a speeding car ran the red light and plowed right into them. The Babcock boy went right through the windshield head first onto the frozen pavement and was killed instantly. Others, including Darrell, were strewn over the pavement and were unconscious. The girls in the other cars came and spread their coats over them, then waited anxiously for the ambulance. Darrell's tongue was almost bitten in two, and he had to stay in the hospital for three days. He wrote, "And there I rotted away for three days!" When we got word of the accident, we made contact by ham radio and found that Darrell had left the hospital and was doing well. Mrs. Roy Hamman wrote too.

"Looks like Darrell is going to be all right because he is teasing the girls again!"

We were thankful and praised the Lord, but when we received Darrell's letter, we were even more thankful.

"I had been thinking how nice it would be just to stay in America, make lots of money and live the easy life," he wrote, "but now the Lord has again shown me that my life does not belong to me. So I have dedicated my life to go back to Liberia as a missionary." We praised God!

What a thrill it was then, in 1968, to see him step off a ship in Liberia. When we flew him into Zondo, the people said, "Welcome back home, Darrell!"

"Yes, I have come back home," he agreed. He had been, and was again, a great favorite with all the Bassa people.

Forced Landing

I was flying the superintendent of Bassa County from the coast to his interior farm. On the way, we dropped into our Zondo base for a cup of coffee. Coming in for a landing with the wings level, I checked my gas and saw that I had twice the gas I needed to get me to my supply base at Suakoko. I didn't realize that the gauge read higher than it should. We took off, and I dropped the superintendent on his landing strip and went on.

After about ten minutes, the engine sputtered and died. I was shaken! I looked at the gas gauge: plenty of gas. Was I really out of gas? Then I remembered my emergency tank of one gallon and turned it on. The windmilling prop came back to life, running smoothly. What should I do? Suakoko was still 15 minutes away!

I had only ten minutes left. Well, at least the gallon of fuel would take me to the road. I swung left, and in six minutes I was over the narrow road that disappeared under the overhanging jungles in most places. I could see no way to land on it. However, I did not want to tear up the plane in the jungle, so I prayed and climbed higher. Then the ten minutes were up; the engine quit again; and I knew I had to go down.

"Lord," I prayed, "this is Your airplane, and I am Your servant; would You please preserve us both for a great ministry?" I looked ahead and saw a clearing on the road and a small hut. Maybe I could duck underneath the tall trees and skid to a stop on the road. "Please, Lord, help me now!" I was a bit too high and coming in on a dead stick, so I slipped it violently to cut my airspeed. Down I came through that hole, and just before I touched down, I straightened out and slammed on my brakes. The wheels skidded. The branches caught my wings and really slowed me down. Just before I stopped, however, the right wing cleared. With the left wing still in branches, the plane was pulled into the ditch and the prop bent. I jumped out without a scratch and was praising the Lord when a native man came running to congratulate me. "You do well, Boss! You do well!" A Pan American plane had crashed in that area not too long before, killing the entire crew and all the passengers. Consequently, the local people thought it wonderful that I had lived, and I agreed.

I thanked the man and sent him down the road to stop any oncoming traffic. Then a lot of men came running from the hut. They said, "You do well, Boss." I thanked them, too, then asked one to go in the other direction to stop any traffic. The rest I asked to help me push the plane to the clearing and off the road. We had to chop the branches for the wings to clear as we pushed the plane. When I had it safely off the road, I examined the damage.

In addition to the bent prop, the fabric on the wing tips was torn a bit. But that was all! I took off the prop, and a man gave me a needle and thread so I could sew up the wings. I was so glad to see my friend Fred Helem from Firestone "just happen" to come up the road in his pickup. He gave me a lift to the government machine shop at Suakoko. We carefully worked the prop over until it looked good. Then, taking some gas, we went back to the plane. I bolted the prop back on and tracked it. It was off a bit, but I knew it would get me out of the jungle. I paid the men for widening the road a bit for me and, with the gas in my tank, I slowly taxied under the jungle to the place I had stopped.

Then I turned the plane around by hand and climbed in. Pouring the power to the 115 horses, the plane jumped forward and out through the hole. The prop was a bit rough, so I throttled way back with just enough power to putt-putt slowly above the road till I could reach my supply base at Suakoko. I worked on the prop until it ran smoothly. That night as I got ready for bed, I took my Bible and just let it fall open. It opened at Psalm 50:15: "Call upon me in the day of trouble: I will deliver thee, and thou shalt glorify me." I did, and have been doing it ever since. The Lord is so *good!*

The next morning we communicated with the other missionaries by radio, for by then we had contact with all our stations. Yila came on. "Abe, Dick Miller is very sick. Could you come and fly him out?"

"Roger, Roger. I will be right there as soon as the fog clears," I radioed back. There I was, back in service, even though the wing tips still flapped a bit!

A Downdraft? Oh No!

A Lutheran missionary pulled into Suakoko about 2:00 P.M. and begged me to fly him to Zorzor. I went out and looked at the sky. "OK," I said. "There is one thunderhead way out there, but we will make it long before it comes our way." As soon as we were loaded, we took off. I kept a watchful eye on that black cloud. I never saw a cloud grow so fast, but I felt sure we could make the trip in good time. Nevertheless, I pushed the throttle forward a little. We were almost in sight of the mission when the storm closed in behind us. Just one more steep ridge, and we would glide in for a landing.

But as I came near the ridge, I felt a violent updraft. It was sucking the plane into the clouds, and I saw my altimeter winding upwards. The question came to me, "Could there be a downdraft too?" and then I knew the answer! We were on a fast elevator going down. I gave it full throttle and felt sure I could still cross the ridge. Suddenly palm trees appeared right in front of me, so I kicked the rudder and dove into a ravine. I had a range of hills on either side and a mountain in front of me. What could I do? Well, the wind was on the tail and had to go over the mountain. As it did, it carried us along with it. We got over the ridge, and I let down for a landing at the mission.

The doctor heard me coming, so he raced out to meet me in his jeep. When I turned the engine off, he looked at me and asked, "Abe, why are you so white today?" Isaiah 41:10 came to mind: "Fear thou not; for I am with thee: be not dismayed; for I am thy God: I will strengthen thee; yea, I will help thee; yea, I will uphold thee with the right hand of my righteousness."

The Red Bull

The chief at Yila had a red bull, and red bulls and red airplanes just don't get along together. Everytime we landed at Yila, we had to circle to make sure that bull was out of sight.

One day J. T. Lyons had just landed the Super Cub at Yila when the red bull came charging the red airplane. J. T. loved his airplane just like all of us pilots do, so he did a rather risky but brave thing. He climbed out of the cockpit and stood between the bull and the plane with his fists ready to fight that bull. The bull pawed the ground with his hooves and put his head down, ready to charge that red airplane. But when his eye caught J. T.'s fierce, determined look and his powerful fists swinging around, he backed off. Hurrah for J. T.!

Another time I came in, flying the Tri-Pacer, and landed safely, for the bull was well to the side of the runway. He didn't like that red Tri-Pacer either and stood glowering at it. I loaded my passengers quickly. After my short prayer, with one eye on the bull and the other on the runway, I started rolling for takeoff. I wondered if the bull would charge me, so I applied only medium power because I might have to skid to a stop. But when I passed the point where the bull couldn't catch me, I wondered why we weren't gaining speed. Oops! I forgot! Quick—full throttle! The plane leaped forward, and we cleared the trees, but it was scary. Finally we appealed to the government to pressure the chief to move the bull to another area, which he did, so there was no more bull.

Don't Jump Out of the Plane!

One Sunday evening I approached the Atlantic Ocean, swung around and lined up with the landing strip at Pastor Taa David's church. The church was on the edge of the village, and everyone came to welcome "Teachah Gantah."

As we walked past the church, I noticed it had a new "bell." The old brake drum had not rung well, but this propeller blade rang out beautifully. "Pastor David, God blessed you, for you to have two church bells. But where did you get this new one?" I asked.

"Teachah Gantah, the other day when we were cutting the trees for my rice farm, we found this propeller blade stuck in the ground right in the bush. I don't know where it came from."

"Oh David!" I exclaimed. "That came from my friend's airplane. He came by here the other day, and one propeller blade flew right off. Then the engine shook so bad it almost dropped out."

The pilot had told me his story: "I was flying the coast with two native Methodist preachers in the backseat and a woman beside me. When I lost my prop, the engine nearly dropped out from the shaking, but I got the engine stopped just before it did. The oil lines broke, however, and the oil caught fire. The cowling popped off and hit the windshield, breaking it, which sent smoke pouring into the cockpit. The two men in the back jumped out in midair, and the woman wanted to jump too, but I stopped her. It was unusually quiet then— just the wind whistling past the plane. The smoke was so thick I couldn't even see the instruments. I began to listen to the whistle of the wind. When it got too quiet, I knew we were going into a stall, so I pushed the wheel forward. When it got too loud, I knew we were in a dive, so I pulled back a bit. Slowly we came down, but I could not see a thing until I saw some trees swishing past the window. I pulled the wheel back all the way and landed in the Little Cola River. The plane smashed against the bank, knocking me out temporarily. When I came to, I noticed the door was open, so I climbed out and saw the woman walking away from the plane. I yelled for her to wait for me when suddenly, behind me, the plane burst into flames.

The woman passenger began to call: "Yoooo . . . hoooo . . . !" A woman answered from a nearby farm, and she directed us to her by her calls. We discovered that fortunately we were only a mile from the end of the road. When we crossed the river to the waiting taxi, the driver whisked us to the Buchanan hospital, about 20 miles away."

He concluded his story by pointing his finger up and acknowledging, "Only because of God am I alive!" The two men who jumped out were not found until the next year when the people cut jungle down to make a new farm. All they found were skeletons. The moral of the story: Don't jump out of the plane!

The Doctor with His Bag

It was a hot and windy day, which makes for rough flying, and I had to fly Dr. Schindler up from radio station ELWA near Monrovia to Yila to help our extremely ill nurse, Carolyn Hovingh.

Flying along above the road from the coast and bouncing all over the sky, I noticed my passenger's face begin to pale. "Doc," I hollered, "how'd you like to drop in to Suakoko for a coffee break?" He agreed, thankfully, so I gradually let down for a gentle landing to be kind to his equilibrium!

I taxied to a stop in front of our house and hollered to Susie, "Put the coffee on!" Then to the doctor, "You will feel much better after a little break from that rough flight."

We were eating sandwiches and drinking coffee when I suggested, "You know, Doc, it helps me a whole lot to chew on some pickles when I am woozy. Would you like some?"

"Sure, Abe," he replied. "That sounds good."

"Oh, you know what?" I exclaimed. "I have a new batch of homemade root beer ready. Would you like some?"

"I haven't seen root beer since I left America! Yes, thanks; I will try that too," he responded. There we were, eating sandwiches, drinking coffee, chewing on pickles and enjoying root beer.

"I feel great now," he announced shortly. "I should make it to Yila OK."

"Yes," I agreed. "It's only fifteen minutes; you'll be all right now."

We took off again, and the air was worse than before; we bounced all over the sky. I kept a wary eye on my passenger, and soon I noticed the blood draining from his face again. I passed him a plastic bag.

"If you need it, use it," I instructed him. Pretty soon it all came up: sandwiches, coffee, pickles and root beer. He filled the bag and then did the most amazing thing. He wiped his mouth and turned to me with a grin.

"Good the second time! I just love root beer and pickles!" Most people feel like dying, not joking, when they are airsick. As we landed at Yila, he climbed out, and holding up the bulging plastic bag, greeted the missionaries.

"Here is the doctor with his bag," he joked.

Anytime I see him now, I always ask, "Doc, do you still like root beer and pickles?"

Crossing the Red Sea!

Carolyn Hovingh had worked faithfully and well with the 450 leprosy patients at the Yila Leprosy Colony and had brought healing to many, but her strength was gone. She needed a break badly. On top of all that, her mother was dying. But Carolyn had no peace in her heart about leaving, for who would take care of her beloved people?

The executive committee had a quick meeting and decided that Carolyn had better go home. I came flying into Yila, dodging the worst rainstorms. One had just crossed Yila airstrip, and water stood all over the runway. I landed, with water splashing everywhere. When I shut the engine off, I hollered, "Carolyn, come quickly, because another big rainstorm is coming in fast." She came splashing through the puddles with native boys bringing her bags. In a short time we were loaded.

I started the engine, sped through the puddles and took off, banking sharply to avoid the incoming storm. I took my heading for Roberts Airport to catch Carolyn's flight, and then we saw an amazing thing. There, ahead of us, was a straight clear path in the exact direction we had to go, and on each side was a wall of black heavy rainclouds. As we flew along this corridor, I turned to Carolyn and remarked, "Do you see that? It's like walking through the Red Sea on dry land."

"I see, I see!" she replied over the noise of the engine. "This is God's sign to me that I should go home." She caught her plane and got home to Grand Rapids in time to help her sick mother.

Lightning Strikes at Suakoko

At this time we were stationed at Suakoko, which was known for its frequent thunderstorms. We were quite civilized by then; we had a generator with wires strung all over to the houses and church. We even had a simple telephone system.

Just after I installed it, I called a neighboring missionary, Nadyne Ricks, and while we were talking her houseboy said, "Missy, you can't hear him; no way!"

"Oh yes, I can," she insisted. "Come and listen for yourself." When I spoke to him, he would not answer but just grunted and flopped himself down into a chair.

"Now I believe everything the white man tells me. I believe Jesus died and rose again!" We laughed about that. We talked on the radio every morning and evening, over distances of hundreds of miles, yet this simple device floored him.

On one particular day we heard and saw a thunderstorm coming, and was it a biggy! On it came: rain, wind and lightning, and then the big crash that felt like an earthquake. Minnie Lane, a missionary neighbor across the airstrip, had been standing under her dining room light. The lightning shattered the light bulb, and the clip-on shade hit her head as it fell without breaking. She was frightened and shaking as she came running across the airfield in the darkness with her flashlight. By the time Minnie reached our house, she was crying hysterically.

Our daughter, Suzanne, slept on a steel-frame bed. The current from the lightning leaped out of the electrical socket into the steel frame and paralyzed one of her legs for a while. We figured her leg must have been touching the steel. The generator ran but produced no power, for it had been blown out too. Many wires had been shorted out, so it took me days to repair everything. But the Lord was with us and we could still say, "Great is the LORD, and greatly to be praised . . . !" (Ps. 48:1).

The Intellectual Snake

In Liberia we had many snakes of every color, size and length. We even had an intellectual snake that loved to browse among the schoolbooks. One day Teacher David came running and yelled, "Teachah Gantah, come quick! A long snake is in the bookshelf." I ran over to the school, and there he was, hiding behind the books. Only his head stuck out as he looked us over. I prepared a long stick with a fork on the end of it and then, carefully approaching, jabbed him and held his head fast against the wall. With my machete I began to mash his head until it was reduced to a pulp. Then I let him go. David had been watching from a distance. When that snake came out, thrashing around all over the place, David took one big leap over the school benches and disappeared! After chopping the snake's head off, I knew he wasn't going anywhere, so I wasn't worried.

At another time, Matthew, a Bible school student, had been cutting trees down for his farm. When he put his hand on a branch to cut it, a green mamba, whose color blended perfectly into the color of the branch, bit him on the hand. He quickly made a tourniquet around his arm and walked the 100 yards to our house. I was in bed, sick with malaria. When Susie brought me the sad news, she said, "I just don't know what to do with him. You know that people usually die with a green mamba bite, but maybe it did not hit a vein. Maybe there is hope for him if you think you can get up and fly him to the Uniroyal Rubber Plantation hospital." What to do?

I got dressed and with Susie's help pushed the plane out of the hangar. Matthew slid into the backseat and I into the pilot's seat. Then I kicked the starter, taxied to the end of the runway, checking my instruments as I went, and immediately took off. It was only a five-minute flight, and when I circled the hospital to indicate that I had an emergency, the truck ambulance came to meet me.

The nurse took a good look, then lanced the swollen hand. Out poured a whole bunch of black, ugly-looking stuff. She squeezed it gently, and more putrid poisonous stuff came flowing out. She commented, "God blessed you in that the snake didn't hit your vein, but you'd better stay a few days for observation." Matthew lived, praise the Lord!

A Leper Fell among the Driver Ants

It was one of those days that had begun at 5:30 A.M.—a Bible school class for me to teach at 6:30 and radio contact at 7:00 while I ate breakfast. I was lined up for a full day of flying. But before the fog lifted, enabling me to fly, I had to carry a missionary to the hospital in my VW bus. So I was moving right along.

We turned off the mission onto the main road. Along the way a little farther, I saw a sight I will never forget. A leper who had come through the darkness of the night had slipped in the mud and had fallen right into the path of a great army of driver ants, which had begun to cover his body. In his weakness, he could not get up, but he did take off all his clothes so he could brush the ants off with his hands. He was muddy and bloody, and the ants were deeply lodged all over his body and imbedded in his hair. I said to myself, "He is dirty and bloody. Besides, he's a leper. My bus is clean; the missionary needs to get to the doctor; and it seems as if everybody is waiting for me today. I am so busy; surely someone else will come by and help that poor soul!"

Then I remembered the man in the Bible who had fallen among thieves who left him half dead and bloody. The priest and Levite also were busy and clean; everybody seemed to be waiting for them too, so they passed by on the other side. Then I opened the bus door, carried that filthy, bloody leper to the bus, laid him on the floor and took him to the "inn," a clinic where the medics took care of him. I felt good and went on through a good day. Jesus said of the Good Samaritan, "Go, and do thou likewise." Are you willing to do inconvenient things for Jesus? How about dirty or risky things that might mess up your schedule?

They Stole My Car!!

Going out on the road for meetings in the villages with the public address system and the projector almost every night, I found that my battery took quite a beating. When I came home I would plug in the charger to build up the battery again.

One day my daughter Suzanne and I went to push out the plane for a flight, and it would not move. Then I noticed that my car was gone, but where? Suzanne had been reading a lot of mystery books so she exclaimed delightedly, "A mystery!" and began to practice her sleuthing, much to our amusement.

Not many people in Liberia had a car, and the country had just a few roads. So I took off in the plane in search of my little green Opel. I searched all the local roads, but found nothing. Then, since I had to fly to Monrovia, I followed the road, carefully looking everywhere. On the way back, I spotted the Opel in a ditch at Kakata, about 30 miles down the road. Since the road was wide and no traffic was in sight, I dropped the plane down on it and rolled toward my car. People came from Kakata in great droves to see what had happened, thinking I had crashed. I walked over to examine my car. It had not been damaged; but it was out of gas, the battery was dead, and did it ever stink from the goats the thieves had hauled in it!

A friend who worked with the Peace Corps came along and agreed to drive it home for me. We got some gas and gave it a push. Away he went. I took off and headed for home, bringing the good news to Susie. The Opel came home that evening. Then I painted a big white spot on top of the roof of the car so that if there was a next time, I would be able to "spot" my car more easily!

After that experience, I decided to wire up the mission with an alarm system. Since my generator started at the flip of a switch, I put toggle switches above all the outside doors. Any one of them would start the generator, which would produce a series of lights all over the place. The thieves would come through the screen windows, then open all doors for a quick getaway in case we woke up. I figured that commotion should scare them off, and it did.

One night the light in our bedroom, right over our heads, came on. Susie woke up with a start and whispered tensely, "Abe, there is a thief in the house!" I awoke, took my gun and eased out of the bedroom. Then I heard the back screen door slam shut, and I knew the thief was gone. I ran to my car and spun all around the mission with it but saw no sign of anyone. However, our clothes and other things the thief had grabbed were strewn everywhere. Mary Lou Rhodes' car had been broken into and the wires crossed, but the thieves didn't have enough time to get away.

I took three Bible school men to the main road where a shortcut path led from the mission to the town. I gave them my shotgun and flashlight and told them, "If you hear someone come, shine the light in his eyes and shoot the gun into the air." They hid in the bush. Soon they heard some footsteps, then they shined the bright light into the intruder's eyes and pulled the trigger—BANG! The thief threw off his raincoat and, stark naked, jumped into a thornbush and disappeared. When the Bible school men returned, they were laughing.

"Teachah Gantah, we know that man will pick thorns off his body for the rest of the night!"

We passed the word around that the whole mission was electrified and that the car horn would blow if you so much as opened a door. We had no more trouble after that!

The Unholy Ax

At Suakoko, as we continued to plant the seed of the Word of God, souls came to the Lord in great numbers. One young man came to me and said, "Teachah Gantah, my heart troubles me too much! I know Jesus is in my heart; but before I believed, I did something bad. I was working for the LAMCO Iron Ore Mining Company helping build the railroad. The ax I was working with felt so good in my hand. I began to think it would be fine too much to have that ax to cut down the trees for my farm. One day when it was time to knock off (quit) and no one was looking, I threw that ax into the bush. Then after dark, I went back there, picked it up and took it home. Now every day I look at that ax, my heart troubles me too much. What should I do?"

"I know what to do," I replied without hesitation. "Bring the ax. We will fly over there and return it to them."

He brought the ax. We climbed into the airplane, fired it up and took off. In 12 minutes we were circling to land on the LAMCO Company's strip. It was a short walk to the office of operations. We walked into the big building, into the large room of desks and people. Everyone was looking at us as I asked, "Who is the big man here?"

"I am," said one of the men. We went over to him and laid the ax on his desk. Then I explained the situation.

"This man Flumo worked for you. One day he stole this ax. Now he has believed on Jesus, so he wants to return it and begs you to forgive him." All eyes were riveted on us. Each person had a look of astonishment on his face, and a great quietness came over the place. Finally the "boss" spoke:

"Thank you; we forgive you." We turned and walked out. What a testimony, in a small way like what Zacchaeus did in Luke 19:1–10. I believe we ought to follow his example and show in a real way to the world that we are changed people.

Doaita Crash

I had just overhauled the engine completely and spent several hours test-flying it over the station. Then I landed and asked my boys to gas up the airplane while I went to have lunch. "Did you fill the tank?" I asked when I returned.

"Yes, Teachah," they replied. I stuck my finger into the tank; it was indeed full.

Now for my first flight of some supplies to Doaita for the Karl Luybens. On the end of the runway I checked all instruments carefully and had a word of prayer. Then I took off. Everything felt good, and the engine had great power and was running smoothly. I was pleased as I greased it into the short strip. I greeted the Luybens, delivered their supplies and visited a bit.

Then we said "so long," and I taxied to the end, swung around and took off. I was practically empty of cargo, so I was airborne in no time. But then suddenly the engine quit cold. I bounced back onto the end of the runway, rolled right off the end, down the hill into an old overgrown rice farm, burst through an old fence and plowed into stumps with my landing gear. I got stopped with my right wing up against a tall stump. The soldier in the backseat, who had asked for a ride, screamed with fright, so I let him out first. Then I crawled out through the underbrush beneath the wing and saw John Mark Luyben come running down the hill with tears streaming down his cheeks. "Uncle Abe, I am sorry, I am so sorry!"

"John, I am so sorry too," I replied, with tears in my eyes also.

When the chief heard of the crash, he ran into the jungle to hide, for he knew the government would hold him responsible for any death in his town. Others ran after him, however, and told him the good news that nobody had died.

People came and wanted to help, so we began to clear away the brush. I lifted up the right wing and propped it up with a pole, then tied the tail down. I checked for damage. My right landing gear was gone, my nose wheel demolished, my propeller bent; and the right wing had a deep dent from the tall stump.

But what had caused the engine to quit? The first thing I suspected was dirty gas. Sure enough, when I removed the gasculator, I found it filled with junk. But where had it come from? We always strained all our gas through a chamois skin. Later I learned that the boys had pumped the gas straight from the drum without straining it.

The next day Harlan Rahilly came to my rescue and, with the Super Cub, flew me to Monrovia to my friend Bill deMush, who had five Tri-Pacers in his air taxi business. I walked into his place, told Bill the sad story and pointed to his only spare landing gear, hanging on the ceiling. "Bill, I need that." He pointed out the door toward his planes.

"Abe, do you see that line-up of airplanes? If I have an accident, I will need it too."

"Please, Bill," I pleaded, "then just lend it to me to get my plane out of the jungle." He was quiet for a while and then spoke up.

"Abe, maybe if I let you have it, God will bless me and I won't have an accident." He let me buy it, and he didn't have an accident.

God Put a Hole in the Clouds for Me

One night when I was sound asleep, there came a knock at my door about midnight. I stirred and muttered to Susie, "Now who could that be? It must be a white man." (Our national people don't knock; they say "bock bock.") As I opened the door I saw two white men.

"Are you the pilot, sir?" they asked.

"Yes," I answered.

"Well sir, we have a man at the road building site who is in very bad condition with a heart attack. Would you come and pick him up at 6 A.M. at Belefonai and fly him to Firestone [the rubber plantation]?"

"6:00 A.M.!" I exclaimed. "That is when the fog is the worst!"

"Would you please try, sir?" they pleaded. "We will run down the road to meet you at Roberts Airport and take him to the hospital from there."

"OK," I replied, "I will try," and went back to bed.

I got up early and filled both gas tanks to keep me flying in case I got stuck above the fog. I knew that in the dry season the fog would burn off in a few hours. As soon as I took off, I faced a thin layer of fog. The farther I went, the thicker it became. I checked my time and started counting the minutes (I knew it was a ten-minute flight), holding my compass-heading steady. Then the beautiful sun began to peek above the clouds and grew until it flooded the sky. Below me floated a gorgeous, fluffy, snow-white expanse of clouds as far as my eye could see, and I praised the Lord for His glory. "Lord," I prayed, "this is glorious, but I will need a hole in the clouds in three minutes. Would you please make a hole for me?" I was still counting. Eight minutes passed, then nine. At that point I saw a darker area ahead. At ten minutes I came to that God-given hole and the airfield directly below me. I breathed a prayer: "Thank You, Lord!" as I dove down through the hole and slipped in for a landing.

The doctor was waiting for me with his patient and thanked me for coming. The patient was a big man, so I took out the backseat of the Tri-Pacer, placed the cushions on the floor and laid him on them. The doctor brought a welding tank of oxygen, attached a hose, slipped a plastic bag over the man's head and, opening the valve, began to give him oxygen. We climbed aboard. "Are you ready?" I asked the doctor.

"Yes, sir," he said. So we had our usual word of prayer, took off and climbed through that hole again, up above the clouds where it was unusually smooth sailing. I took my heading for Roberts Airport, and in an hour we landed there. Those two men were there waiting for us. We lost no time in transferring patient and doctor to the pickup, with the Firestone doctor and me following by car.

The patient's lungs were nearly full of fluid, so they had him sitting up in the back of the pickup. About halfway there, the oxygen ran out, and they began to speed up. When they arrived at the hospital, the doctor shouted for someone to bring a tank of oxygen. They did, but when they hooked it up, it was empty. Then they brought a second tank, but it was empty too. Quickly they rushed a third tank to the gasping man, but it was too late; he had stopped breathing. The last words I heard him say were, "Oh Lord Jesus!"

"Whosoever shall call upon the name of the Lord shall be saved," states Romans 10:13. We were brought so close to eternity that day that neither the doctor nor I spoke on the way back. "And as it is appointed unto men once to die, but after this the judgment" (Heb. 9:27).

30th Anniversary Crash

In 1966 we moved back to Zondo to work among the Bassa people again. Roy Watkins and J. T. Lyons were the pilots at Tappi station. I was down at Zondo, about 70 miles closer to the ocean. We had the Rocket Maule and the Super Cub airplanes. We would switch planes back and forth to suit our needs.

J. T. took the Maule to Monrovia while I flew the Super Cub there, and we exchanged planes. It was Susie's and my 30th anniversary. I knew a great dinner and a good time awaited me at Zondo. I had bought six pretty long-stem drinking glasses as a gift for Susie. With the glasses, some supplies and two bags of cement on board, I took off for home.

I was about ten miles out when I began to experience an engine slowdown. As I put on the gas booster pump, the power came back. Soon, however, the engine began to slow down again. By that time I was over the swamp near the ocean opposite the radio station ELWA. I wondered if I should try to land in the middle of the swamp—which looked quite solid. However, the power came surging back, and I dismissed that thought. Then the engine slowed down again. I was heading for the trees. Not wanting to crash into the trees, I turned back to the swamp. I was still in the turn when I lost all my power and the plane dropped heavily on the left wheel. A small shrub caught my left wing, spinning me off to the side, and the plane slid for 100 feet on firm ground until it finally stopped. Escaping without a scratch, I jumped out.

Then I heard gasoline pouring out. A stick had jammed my quick-drain valve open. I pulled it out, and the flow stopped. By that time a puddle of gas had collected under the plane, but no spark, thank God! I stood beside my crippled bird. It looked so sad with drooping wings, washed-out landing gear and a prop that looked like a cork-screw.

I stood there with an indescribable feeling. What was I doing down here? It seemed like I should have gone up to Glory. For days that feeling lingered with me.

Anyway, I walked through the swamp and caught a ride to our mission headquarters in Monrovia, where the radio carried the bad *and* the good news to Susie.

Albert Ostrander and Dr. Smith, our doctor from Yila who happened to be in the city, took me through the swamp and back to the plane in Albert's four-wheel-drive Land Rover. When Doc saw the plane, he looked me over. "Are you sure you're all right, Abe?" he asked dubiously.

"Yes, Doc," I confirmed. "Praise God, I don't even have a scratch." We took out the bag of cement, the drinking glasses that weren't even chipped, the battery and the radio, then left the crippled bird to sleep in the swamp.

The next day J. T. Lyons joined us, for he was on vacation at ELWA, and we began the salvage work. Some natives carried out the wings on their heads. The fuselage was rolled out on the tail wheel by six men carrying and pushing on a timber stuck through the engine mount. The engine was carried out on the Land Rover. Everything finally got out to the Monrovia airfield and into a hangar. There we determined that the cause of the accident had been a faulty gas line switch that had not allowed gas through.

J. T. Lyons and his son Sandy, along with my son Darrell and I, began the restoration work. We welded, straightened, riveted and painted. With a new prop and landing gear, we finally had it ready to fly again. J. T. wanted to fly it first, so I agreed. "OK. You have worked so hard—take it up."

He taxied out, checked everything carefully and, with those 215 horses pulling mightily, he swooped up into that sunny, beautiful, blue sky. What a wonderful sight to behold! We watched him going through different maneuvers and rejoiced that the big bird was well again. J. T. was all smiles as he taxied in, but then—trouble!

The airport had a big cement obstruction. It served no useful purpose and sat right in the middle of the approach to the hangar. It was on J. T.'s blind right side, and he was heading straight toward it! We hollered, screamed and waved, trying to stop him. Nevertheless, we could not get his attention, and he slowly taxied right into it. With three or four sharp clanking sounds, that beautiful new prop was ruined. J. T. got out of the Maule and sat down on the pavement with his legs crossed and his head in his hands. We gathered around him and felt just as bad as he did. After a while he stood up and said, "Well, praise the Lord anyway!" That was J. T.!

The air taxi owners gathered around too, feeling bad, just as we did, for they were our friends, though unsaved. One piped up, "I have a spare prop I will lend you till you get another from home." We thanked him and knew that Romans 8:28 would prove its truth again somehow!

Then amazing things began happening in our churches. A faction had broken away from our Zondo church, but they called me to go into their church for a time of thanksgiving. One man stood up and spoke a parable: "That mountain here at Zondo, we know that all the rivers come from that mountain. If that mountain were destroyed, what would happen to all the rivers? We all give thanks to God that you did not die." The people in the outstations called us to come for thanksgiving feasts. All in all, it was a beautiful experience. Churches at home kindly helped pay for the repairs, and we were back in business for the Lord. God is so good!

Darrell and Donna's Wedding

In May 1971, we returned from furlough, and Darrell announced his wedding plans for the end of June. But the Super Cub had been in a crash. How could we do without it? J. T. Lyons and Darrell had spent many hours in rebuilding it at Nimba, and it was nearly ready for the final assembly. We lost no time: day after day, from before breakfast till late at night we worked. Finally, one night it was ready.

Before breakfast, at the crack of dawn, I started it up and taxied down the long field. I had decided just to lift it off a bit and try it out, but when it skimmed along the ground so nicely, I pulled back on the stick and climbed up beautifully. That day, because I didn't have full confidence in the plane yet, I flew it down the railroad tracks all the way to Gay Peter and then cut in toward Zondo. Darrell came in the other plane from Tappi. Then we made the final touchups, painted it and took a trip to Monrovia for the relicensing. We had no problems with the officials, so we were ready for the big wedding.

It was a wonderful day! People came, walking for miles (and some even for days) to see this great sight, to see their special friends, "Teachah Darrell" and "Missy Donna," being married the white man's way. The sky buzzed with airplanes bringing in missionaries and even Donna's folks. They came all the way from New Hampshire! The church was full, and as I "tied the knot," recordings were made for radio station ELWA so all Liberia could hear too. Then came the handshakes and congratulations and a big feast of rice and goat soup in the hangar, which had been cleared out. My wife Susie had baked a beautiful big wedding cake. As the day closed and some rains began moving in, the missionaries took off for home. Then Darrell came to me: "Dad, would you fly Donna and me to the road so we can go on a honeymoon, please?"

"Sure, son," I replied. "Bring your baggage," and soon we took off and dropped them at Gay Peter. For a few days we didn't know where they were, but our people happened to see them. They told us Darrell and Donna were right close by in a suite at the rubber plantation, being waited on hand and foot.

Hugged by a Python

A young man and his wife and children came to the church regularly. They were fine Christians. One day the wife said, "Zoga, please go into the jungle and find some meat for dinner." So Zoga took his machete and, wearing just a loincloth, went forth. In the dark shadows, under the tall trees, the animals could not see Zoga's black skin. They couldn't hear him either, for he knew how to walk stealthily.

After a while Zoga came upon a large squirrel sitting on a branch too high for him to reach. Now Zoga wished he had brought his bow and arrows. Zoga kept watching the squirrel though, and it went into strange antics. It would point its nose straight down, jump up and down, chatter loudly and then point its nose straight down again. Zoga decided the squirrel was trying to tell him something. "There must be some big meat down there," he thought. So he sneaked up right under the squirrel, watched where he was pointing his nose and then began to slash around in the undergrowth. On the third cut Zoga slashed right into the tail of a big, long python. He froze.

That snake was so fast that before Zoga knew what was happening, he was being tied up as the python whipped itself around his body. The machete dropped from his right hand, but praying hard, he was able to retrieve it quickly. By then Zoga's left hand was pinned down. The head of the big snake loomed in front of his face. The snake looked right at him, its mouth wide open. Later, Zoga told me, "Teachah, I could see his big teeth, and I was so scared because I knew I was done for, unless God helped me. I cried out to God and began to slash around, chopping and chopping until finally I was able to chop his head right off. The big snake began to relax, and I stepped out of the deadly coil. I said, 'Thank You Jesus! Thank You Jesus!' "

He grabbed the big head and began to run, over the big log that crossed the river and right into the village. Some of the village people saw him coming and were stunned. He ran right to the chief's house and hollered, "Look my people; see what I got! Follow me." The whole village—men, women and children—ran after him, across the big log and into the deep jungle.

When they saw the long snake, they were amazed. It was still twitching a little. "How did you manage to kill such a big snake?" they asked.

"When it tied me up and was going to squeeze the life from me, I began to call upon Jesus. He gave me strength to kill it with this machete." About ten men lifted the long snake onto their heads, and they began to chant as they slowly marched forward, swaying from side to side.

"Zoga, Zoga, Zoga went into the bush. He met this big snake. It tried to kill him, but he had his machete and with a prayer and the power of Jesus, he slew it." Across the log they came, still chanting, slowly marching right into the village. They did not stop until they were at the chief's door. He stood up from his big chair, unfolded his chief's gown and with his elephant's tail in his hand came to stand beside Zoga. While the men stretched the snake out in the middle of the village, Zoga looked at the chief. He could tell what the chief wanted. So Zoga took his machete and chopped off a nice big piece for him. Then more and more pieces were cut until everyone in the village had snake steak that day!

Do you get the lesson? That old serpent, the Devil, also walks about seeking whom he may devour. You are no match for him. When you begin to play with sin, he is happy to put a rope around you until he has you hopelessly tied up. But even at the last minute, if you call on the Lord Jesus Christ and have the sword of the Spirit, which is the Word of God, help is available for you. "Wherefore take unto you the whole armour of God . . . and the sword of the Spirit, which is the word of God" (Eph. 6:13, 17).

Saved So As by Fire

Zondo station was far removed from any main road. One day after the sun had just gone down, four men, carrying a man in a hammock, appeared. The man had been so badly burned that his flesh hung in shreds from his body.

The man had gone to his farm, together with his two grown sons, to burn the bush they had cut down for his new farm. But since there was no wind, the man sent the sons back to the village. After they had departed, he lingered behind. Then a nice breeze began to blow, so he quickly lit his long bamboo torch. Starting from the upwind side, he began to set fire to the dry branches, hopping just ahead of the blaze that by then was reaching for the sky. Suddenly he had an epileptic attack, falling down in convulsions. The fire passed right over him. His sons, seeing the smoke rising high in the sky, came running to help. But they could not see him through the smoke. He finally came to and cried out for help, so they ran through the smoke and fire and brought him out to the mission.

I was stunned. What should I do? It would be dark in no time, and our planes were not equipped for night flying. As I looked up into the sky, I saw a large, high cumulus cloud. The sun was still beautifully reflecting from it. I yelled, "Bring him quickly!" as I ran to push the plane out from the hangar.

As soon as we were on board, I gunned the throttle, raced to the end of the runway, swung around and took off. I needed five minutes to make it to the plantation hospital, so I sped full throttle all the way. I swung around the hospital once, pushing my throttle back and forth to indicate an emergency. It was nearly dark by the time I buzzed low over my friend's house and banked to land. I could see car lights coming from everywhere as I rolled to a stop.

"What happened, Abe?" they all asked.

"See for yourself," I answered, as the ambulance loaded the man for a quick trip to the hospital. He had third-degree burns over 50 percent of his body and lingered only a week before he died. But that was long enough for a Christian male nurse to lead him to the Lord. Praise God!

On another day I glided into another village to preach. The native medical "dresser" (who went from village to village helping the sick) came running. Behind him in a hammock lay a patient with his neck all taped up. "We beg you, Teachah Gantah," the dresser began. "Oh please help us again. This man tried to kill himself. He cut his throat, but I taped it all up and the blood is stopped. You are the only one who can save him."

"OK," I replied, "I will take him to the hospital where they will take care of him. Thank you for what you did."

At the hospital the medics did a commendable job of sewing him up. While he was in the hospital, one of our Christian male nurses led him to the Lord as well. Two weeks later, he and his father came walking through the mission on their way home and stopped to thank me for giving life to him and eternal life to both of them.

Tappi station called me on the radio to fly a woman who could not deliver her baby. It happened just before the rains when all the people burn their farms in preparation for planting. The sky was black with smoke. After landing at Tappi, I removed the backseat so the woman could lie down and another woman could sit beside her to care for her. It was nearing evening, and there was so much smoke I could just barely see to fly. When I neared Ganta, I ran into a rainstorm, and that, plus the smoke, brought my visibility to near zero. However, I managed to fly on.

Then the whole airplane began to shake and move back and forth. It was weird! I had never felt such a forward and backward motion before and could not figure out what was happening. Then I heard a cry from behind me and, glancing back, I saw that the woman was in convulsions. Then I understood, for a small plane is easily moved around when suspended in thin air. I pressed on, landed in a few minutes and placed the patient into the hands of the good doctor.

Unfortunately we were not always able to save our patients. One day I took a leprous woman from Yila to the hospital in Ganta, but as I approached Ganta, she breathed her last and died. The good doctor came, checked her out and pronounced her dead. "You might as well take her back to Yila," he said, so I turned around and flew her back to our Dr. Smith.

That night in prayer meeting at Zondo, I told the young people about it. They all gasped. "Teachah, who was in the airplane with you when you flew that dead woman?"

"It was just me and the Lord."

"Oh!" they all exclaimed. "We could never do that." Liberians are afraid of dead bodies, thinking the spirit is still around and might harm them. I am so glad that God has not given us the spirit of fear. "I will fear no evil: for thou art with me . . ." (Ps. 23:4).

Teachah Gantah, God Is So Wonderful!

The day had been long: flying, helping people, and now, with the sun dropping to the horizon, I was still far from home. As I passed over Pastor Jeremiah's town, I could see his church in the middle of the village. I thought, "Why not drop in, preach and spend the night with this dear brother?" When he saw the wing dip, Pastor Jeremiah knew I was landing.

"Teachah Gantah is coming to fall down—o!" (land). He ran to meet me. As I rolled up the hill toward the village, he met me and asked, "Teachah Gantah, you will sleep here and preach for us?"

"Yes," I replied, "on one condition: that you let me sleep on my airplane cushions on your floor."

"No way," he protested. "You will never sleep on my floor. You will sleep in my best bed."

"Then I am going," I retorted. "Good-bye."

"Wait! Wait!" he called. "Why do you want to sleep on the floor?"

"Because you don't even have enough beds for your family," I explained. "Just roll a grass mat on the floor, and my cushions will make a wonderful bed for me."

After I had made it all up with the mosquito net hanging over the cushions, he still said, "I don't like it; I don't like it."

His family served me a lovely native dinner, and then we went to the church. Again with the aid of my battery and projector, I showed some Bible filmstrips to a full church. Finally we retired for the night. It was quiet except for the jungle creatures that were tuning up for their nightly concert—so weird and yet so beautiful. After prayer I just closed my eyes, and my tired body dropped off into a deep sleep till morning.

But something happened that night. An army of black driver ants, millions of them, came marching into the pastor's house as I slept. They entered through cracks around the door and the windows and came over the wall. Pastor Jeremiah knew the best thing was to move back, so he stood in the middle of his house with his family.

These ants, though exceptionally small, can carry away people, animals and big python snakes, a little piece at a time! Before a python crushes and swallows a deer, it will go all through the jungle to make sure no driver ants are around. If he makes a mistake, and they find him, they will carry him and the deer away, a little piece at a time. When the ants go into a house, they will clean up all the bugs, rats and snakes that happen to be in the thatched roof.

Pastor Jeremiah began to pray, "Oh Father in Heaven, You know my missionary is sleeping on the floor and these driver ants are moving fast. I pray in Jesus' name, please make them go back, Lord— in Jesus' name, please?"

The next morning he told me the story of how he had prayed. Then he exclaimed, "Teachah Gantah, God is wonderful! After I had prayed awhile, I opened my eyes, and I saw all those drivers turn around and march out. Truly our God is wonderful!"

"Yes, truly our God is wonderful," I responded. What wonderful children of God came out from among our simple tribal people, who trust Him with such childlike faith!

Who Shot Me?

Matthew, one of our Zondo Bible School students, went into the jungle with his shotgun because his family needed some meat. He built a nest in a tree, where he could sit and wait for a deer to come by. While he sat there and waited, another hunter came along and spotted him. Mistaking him for an animal, the other hunter took aim with his shotgun and fired, hitting Matthew.

"Who shot me?" he yelled, whereupon the hunter fled into the village, hid his gun and pretended nothing had happened.

Matthew was wounded, but fortunately most of the pellets missed him and, though bleeding, he was able to walk into the village and present himself to the chief. The chief immediately called the elders together, and they collected all the guns from the village. The chief then asked one of the elders to smell the barrels of the eight guns. Finally the elder decided.

"It is this one; it was fired today."

The gun belonged to a man named Joe. They locked a heavy logging chain around his waist. He was in jail, and that chain was the jail. Where could he go with that long chain dragging behind him? Everybody would know he was a criminal. He had to drag that chain around day and night until Matthew's wounds had healed and then the palaver (case) would be settled. Through this incident Matthew led Joe to the Lord, and they became brothers in the Lord.

What a Letdown!

Chick Watkins was flying the Super Cub, carrying a sick man to the hospital. As he returned to Tappi, his left wing slowly lost its lift. He kept pushing the control stick farther and farther to the right to hold up that left wing, and he began to wonder if he would make it home. Still it was dropping. Eventually the stick was all the way to the right; would he make it in safely? By using a little right rudder, he got just enough lift to slip over the last tall trees and glide in safely. His heart pounded as he rolled to a stop in front of the hangar, but he exclaimed, "Praise God, He brought me in safely!" as he opened the cockpit.

The big question, as always, was, What had happened? When Chick looked on the top of the wing, he noticed loose fabric and collapsed ribs. On removing an inspection plate, he saw that the linen stitch cords that hold the fabric to the ribs were all gone, chewed off. That night he called me on the radio and told me the story: "I think a little mouse got into the wing and chewed off all the cords," he explained. "Would you please come and help us out?"

The next morning I flew over and, after praying for wisdom, we decided to cut the whole top cover open from the back and fold it over the front. Then we began sewing it back together from the inside, doping and taping it, then pulling and applying more dope (a thick liquid or pasty preparation). After a lot of patient hard work, it tightened up nicely, and we were back in business for the Lord.

Another pilot, J. T. Lyons, experienced that letdown feeling but with a different cause. With 100 percent humidity and the heat from the exhaust, our mufflers did not last long. J. T. was bringing four preachers back to Tappi when he began to lose power but was able to limp into Zika airstrip, just making it in over the trees. As soon as J. T. was on the ground, he praised the Lord. But again: What had happened? When J. T. started the plane again, he had full power, so assuming he had had carburetor ice, he decided to go home.

With full power, J. T. took off and was nicely airborne when the engine quit cold. He bounced on the end of the strip, and the plane leaped over tall stumps at the end, settling into soft new growth. The people came and literally carried the plane by hand over the stumps back onto the runway. Amazingly, there was no damage to the plane.

J. T. called me to help him troubleshoot. I decided to drop the exhaust stacks. When we started up the plane, we had full power. The middle baffle in the muffler had come loose and was opening and closing the muffler like the butterfly in a carburetor. We decided to run two exhaust pipes directly out, thus eliminating the muffler, so we had no more trouble with that.

Oops, I Forgot!

Gordon and Jean Blair from Seattle wrote to announce, "We are coming to visit you on April 1, 1977."

"We are expecting you," I wrote back, but I failed to write it on my calendar. Imagine the shock and frustration of arriving in a third-world country, not knowing where you were going and being surrounded by a horde of young people, all grabbing for your suit-cases and expecting a tip for carrying them for you. The Blairs managed to fend them off, and while Jean hung onto the baggage, Gordon went to find help. Missionary John Lacy had told the Blairs to contact a man at the hotel just in case I didn't show up to meet them. The man guided them to missionary Ron McCain, who then drove them to Buchanan to be with our son Darrell, his wife, Donna, and Ellie Munter that night. They were in the midst of trying to move to another house in the mud and pouring rain, but Gordon and Jean pitched right in and helped. On the radio that evening they called me—and was my face *red!!* The next morning I picked them up and took them to Zondo.

It was so good to have them there. Our people immediately loved them. Jean even took over a lot of the kitchen work because Susie had a badly infected and swollen foot. Susie insisted she had to take her Bible class at school, so we rolled her over in our two-wheeled cart, equipped with airplane tires.

One day I took the Blairs for a sight-seeing trip. We stopped in a village that had a Devil-bush school right on the edge of the village. Behind the fence of palm branches the people were tapping a rhythm on a turtle shell and singing softly. Finally, a girl, wearing only a grass skirt, came out. I asked her if she would get dressed so my friends could take her picture. She ran into the hut and came out with a string of beads around her neck in addition to the grass skirt. She felt perfectly dressed up!

We flew on and finally landed at the iron ore camp in the back part of Liberia. Since it was the Blairs's 25th wedding anniversary, I took them into the lovely company dining hall, where we celebrated. Sitting around the beautiful table, I told them about my friend, Lloyd Snyder, a missionary with Worldwide Evangelistic Crusade with whom we had eaten in Monrovia. As we ate the dessert of ice cream, a luxury hard to come by in the early days, Lloyd, a man with a real sense of humor, joked, "If this is crusading, I am all for it!" It struck me funny, for Crusade was part of their mission's name, and they were expected to rough it for the Lord. Ever since, when we get together with the Blairs and eat in a nice place, we remind each other, "If this is crusading, I am all for it," and have another good laugh!

From there I took the Blairs to the leprosy colony at Yila. Gordon and I went to see Pastor Enoch, who years before had crawled on his hands and knees for three days to the mission, seeking healing. By the time he arrived, his hands and knees were all bloody and cut from the sharp rocks on the path. As he heard the Word, at first he tried to hide from it. But one day after he heard the bell ring for church, he heard the choir sing, "Don't be too late when the bell rings in Heaven," and it made him think. He did not want to be lost. Not long after, he trusted the Lord Jesus. What a man of God he became!

He went all out for Jesus, and his life was completely trans-formed. He had had one chicken, which he sold to buy a Bible. Then he taught himself to read and immersed himself in the Book. Even though he had no fingers, he managed to turn the pages with the stumps he still had. His eyes were bad and finally he lost one, but he graduated from Bible school. He then became the pastor for the leprosy patients, and all the other pastors looked to him as their example.

As we entered his little house, though by now he was completely blind, he recognized me immediately by my voice and called me by name. "Teachah Gantah, come in. Welcome, welcome!" I told him I had brought my good friend from America to see him and introduced them. Just picture him sitting on the edge of his simple native bed, blind, no fingers, no toes, nose almost gone, face all wrinkled up from leprosy, but smiling from ear to ear. "Brother Blair, thank you for coming to see me," he said. "I am so happy I am saved, and I have much joy in heart because I know Jesus. He is close to me all the time. Oh, it is so wonderful to be a child of God. He takes such good care of me; I just can't help but love Him and praise Him." The scene was too much for tenderhearted Gordon. A tear came rolling down his cheek and a question rose in his heart:

"How can this man in all his poverty and debilitation be so happy?" He was taping the conversation and played it back to his church and friends at home. The unmistakable lesson is that joy does not come from things, but from the love of Christ—joy unspeakable and full of glory.

The Train Crash!

After I had made the survey flight for the LAMCO Iron Ore Mining Company, they built a wonderful railroad all the way from the coast to the mountains of iron ore (about 90 percent pure) in the back corner of Liberia. When the camps for the workers were filled with people, our missionary men put on three weeks of open-air revival meetings, a different team serving each week. We had great crowds, and the Lord blessed with many souls saved. As a result of that push, two churches developed. J. T. Lyons, one of our pilots, agreed to go there as pastor. He built a lovely church with the help of Bob Place, a short-term builder from Michigan. When J. T. went on furlough, Les and Jane Zerbe took over, and the work continued to grow.

One day two Englishmen had flown into the airport ten miles out.

They called Jane for a ride into town because Les had gone flying. With her daughter beside her, Jane chased out there in their Peugeot to pick up the men. On the way back, they approached a railroad crossing. Those interesting Englishmen were such good talkers that, during one glance back at them, Jane plowed right into the oncoming train. The train tore the engine right out of the car and spun the car around. Though they were all tossed around and bruised, no one was seriously hurt. What a miracle! God had again watched over His own. When Les came home and looked the car over, he could not believe they had escaped with just some bruises. God is so good!

Ouch! You Cut My Foot Off!

It had been a long hard day of constant flying, and I was tired. I was glad that in ten minutes I would land at Yila and rest there for the night. Then the radio crackled in my earphones. "FOX TROT NOVEMBER!" (My plane's registration number was FTN.) "Abe, are you there?"

"Yes, what is it?"

"This is Tappi. We have an emergency."

Two schoolgirls had gone into the cassava patch to dig cassava (a root vegetable). While they were digging up the roots, one of the girls suddenly spotted a big cassava snake hidden in the grass, close to the foot of the other girl. Like a flash she slashed out at the snake with her machete but missed. Instead the wide blade went right into the foot of the other girl, nearly cutting it off. She was bleeding badly, they said. I wearily turned my plane toward Tappi and opened up the throttle as I prayed for strength and help for this dear girl.

They brought her to the plane with a blood-soaked, still oozing bandage on her foot. We wasted no time loading her into the plane and, with a helper on board, I was on my way full throttle, keeping an eye on my instruments to watch for overheating. In 25 minutes I was buzzing over the hospital.

The hospital had no airfield, but one day I had noticed the road running through the town had been widened so I thought I would try to land there. I circled and buzzed until I had the attention of all. As I approached for a landing, everything was just right, so I dropped in and rolled to a stop. The people were excited, and I was so happy that we could bring our sick right to the door of the hospital. Unfortunately there was one dog that did not like my airplane—he would run out and try to bite the tires. So when I saw him coming, I would gun the throttle and circle around again. Then, when I came back in, I would hold the plane up until I passed him. Finally, since I still had room, I would land. I had to watch for him on every landing. This time he was nowhere to be seen, so we landed immediately. In no time the girl was whisked off to the doctor and good care.

The sun was going down, but I had just enough time to make it to Yila. As the rosy disk slipped beneath the horizon, I dropped into Yila for the night. "Thank You, Lord, for a good day, for the airplane and for Your protecting hand," I prayed. As I walked into the house, it was radio time and Zondo was calling.

"Where is Abe?" Susie was asking, anxiously.

"Yila to Zondo, Yila to Zondo. Abe is here, Susie," they responded, smiling at me. "All is well." Praise God!

Three Sheep Die for the Old Lady

I was coming in for a landing on one of those tight, narrow and short airstrips. To make matters even worse, the trees on the end had grown rather tall. To land close to the end of the short field I had to dip one wing, kick the rudder and go into a kind of skid, which drops the plane very quickly; we call it "slipping."

I had done that and was straightening out the plane to touch down when a flock of sheep darted out from behind an eight-foot anthill and across my path. I quickly gunned the throttle, pulled back on the stick and thought I had cleared them all, but I heard two thuds. I wondered if I still had wheels, but as I allowed the plane to gently touch down, I began to feel the wheels rolling on the ground. Applying the brakes, I got stopped at the very end. I turned around and taxied to where two sheep were lying upside down with their legs in the air, kicking their last. I jumped out and looked for damage, but couldn't find a scratch. I must have hit them with the tires, and they were dying.

The pastor came and said, "Teachah Gantah, we thank God you didn't die. We thank God your airplane did not spoil, but this is big palaver (trouble). The sheep belong to one old lady (a widow) who we talked to about Jesus. Every time she shakes her head and says, 'I am too old now; leave me alone. I cannot change now. I cannot believe.' How are we going to talk to her now? What can we do?"

"Pastor," suggested one of the believers, "maybe if we all put some money together and give it to the old lady, maybe her heart would sit down small."

"Yes, that is good," I said. "Let us do that." We collected around $15 in silver coins. "Pastor," I said as I was leaving, "in two days I will be back. Please persuade the old lady to stay in town because I want to see her."

Two days later, I came slipping in again, together with a Bible school man. We landed safely and taxied to the pastor's house. The old lady and some others from the village stood beside the pastor. We shook hands, snapped fingers and, when we walked into the pastor's house, the old lady moved to the table. She had tied the silver money in a corner of a long cloth called a "lappa," which the women wrap around themselves to make a skirt. It is a safe place for keys and money when they are tucked into the top fold. Now as she stood by the table, she loosened that pile of money and spread it all over the table. Then she turned to me.

"Teachah Gantah, I cannot take this money. You always come to do good for us and never bad. I will not take the money."

"Old lady (a term of great respect)," I replied, "I hear what you say, but here is a little gift from my wife." I held out some soap, a dress and towels. "Would you take this gift from my wife then?" You should have seen the eyes of that old lady light up! Her hands reached out and, when I placed the gift in her hands, she smiled and was thankful. I saw my chance and said, "Old lady, if you had refused this gift from my wife, you know her heart would have 'fallen way down,' but when I tell her how thankfully you received it, her heart will 'sit down' real good. You know, there is a God in Heaven Who has a gift for you so big that it is hard to understand how wonderful it is. It is called everlasting life. Would you take the gift of God too?"

You should have seen the Bible school man and the pastor as they took over in their excitement and began to preach to her from both sides. I decided the best thing I could do was to pray, so I sat down on the rickety native chair in the corner and prayed, "Father, in Jesus' name, would you please open her heart to your wonderful Word today? Help her to believe and receive the gift of God too."

As I opened my eyes, I saw her hands go out and her head nod up and down as she said, "Yes, I understand. I now receive Jesus and

His wonderful gift of eternal life." Well, it was a time of rejoicing, and I always say that three sheep had to die for the old lady. Somehow, because her own two sheep died, it made sense to her about Jesus, the Lamb of God, dying for her sins and salvation.

When I killed those sheep with the airplane, I thought it was an accident, but as someone said, "It weren't no accident at all; God meant it on purpose." Romans 8:28 had proved itself true again. "And we know that all things work together for good to them that love God."

Is That a Church Bell?

On a Sunday morning I flew into Zika. After the early service, I said to Gaamode, "Brother, come with me and let us fly to Gran Town to preach in Joe's church too." He was enthusiastic, so we took off. In fifteen minutes we landed in Gran Town. As soon as we opened the cockpit, cheers of welcome greeted us. On the ground we were greeted by handshakes and hugs. Before long all the children were chasing after a big rooster for our chicken dinner.

Then the church bell began to ring. It was so clear and beautiful that Gaamode was enthralled by its music. "Brother Joe," he asked, "where did you find that beautiful church bell? It is fine too much— o."

"Brother," Joe responded, "at the sawmill there are plenty to choose from. You could have one too if Teachah Gantah would fly you over there." Gaamode turned excitedly to me.

"Teachah Gantah," he pleaded, "would you please do that for me and my church?"

"You preach for us," I replied, "and as soon as you are finished, we will fly over there so that you can pick out your bell." Was he excited! He preached well, and soon we were in the cockpit ready for takeoff.

The airfield at Gran Town was funny. First I had to check for cows on the field, and then I had to taxi downhill. Next, with full power I would swing around, go back up the hill, go over the hump and shoot down the hill to build up speed. Airborne, I had to climb steadily out over the tall trees and hills.

Well, we made it out of there, and I set the nose of the plane toward the sawmill camp. In about five minutes it came into view. I circled and dropped down for a landing a mile from the camp. In short order we heard the roar of a big unmuffled truck; then we saw it come bouncing out of the jungle toward us with its loose fenders flapping as though it were trying to take off. The native men in the truck were glad to see us.

I greeted them warmly, introduced Pastor Gaamode and told them he would very much like to pick up one of their "church bells." "OK," they said as we all piled into the big truck and roared through the high jungle a mile to the camp and to their "junk pile."

Gaamode was almost beside himself as he tried all the different chunks of iron for sound. He had so many to choose from, and they all sounded sweet. He kept on trying first this one, then that one and then another. Finally he settled on an old oxygen tank that had been discarded because of a leak. He turned to me. "Teachah Gantah, this one is so sweet, but will it be too big to fit into the airplane?"

"Well, Gaamode," I answered, thinking, "we will have to move things around a bit, and you will have to sit on it; but we will make it somehow."

Onto the truck it went. Everybody climbed back in as well, for they wanted to see the airplane fly. We made it back to the airplane and, by rearranging the bananas, the pineapples, the rice and dried monkey meat, we were able to load the "church bell." With the pastor riding on it, we took off, leaving a cloud of dust behind us.

When we arrived safely in Zika with that lovely "church bell," the whole town excitedly turned out to see it. Now everyone, even those in the farms and other villages, would know when it was time for church. What a piece of junk! What a *treasure* for the kingdom of God!

Pastor Gaamode "Eats" a Woman

One time when we had a pastors' conference, Pastor Gaamode had not come. Word came that he had been put in jail in Goah Town, accused of eating a woman. A woman from the town had been missing. Even after 21 days of searching, the villagers had found no trace of her.

They called a woman witch doctor. After her incantations, she spoke. "I saw Pastor Gaamode and three other men eat that woman in the bush and throw her bones into the river." Everybody was shocked.

The soldiers came. They made Gaamode and the three men kneel with their bare knees on sharp gravel holding up their arms above their heads, clasping a broom stick. This was done in the heat of the day, and the men had to face the tropical sun. The soldiers beat them continually and demanded that they confess their guilt, but all four denied it. This went on for days. We dismissed the conference, and all the pastors walked the day-and-a-half journey to be with Gaamode.

The night before they arrived, something wonderful happened. Gaamode told me later, "Teachah Gantah, I suffered too much! So, in jail, together with the other three men, I kneeled down on the dirt floor and prayed to God: 'Oh my Father, are You still with me? My heart troubles me too much. Please encourage my heart.' And then, Teachah Gantah, a bright light shone into our small room—so bright it almost blinded me. It stayed for a while and then disappeared. I said to the other men, 'Did you see the light too?' and they said, 'Yes.' Then I began to preach to them, and right there in the dark jail, I led them to Jesus. Teachah, I was so happy, I began to sing praise to God!"

When daylight came, the woman finally returned to the edge of the village. One man immediately took her to the chief. Then the whole village came to life with great excitement and loud talking. "What is happening in the village?" Gaamode called to a man who was passing the jail.

"The lost woman has returned!" he shouted back.

Then the chief sent the soldiers to release the accused men from the jail, and everybody began to speak kind words to them. When the officials asked the woman why she had hid in the jungle, she explained, "I had a dream that someone was going to kill me, so I hid."

Shortly after that, the pastors arrived, and they began to join in the celebrations. God had answered their prayers, with three souls saved as a bonus. All eighteen pastors locked arms in a long row and began to march round and round the village, singing and praising the Lord! God is wonderful, and He was again glorified through the sufferings of His child.

Two Women Chopped Up!

I was in Monrovia, ready for takeoff, calling the tower for clearance. "Cleared for immediate takeoff," came the response. Then

I heard Susie calling on my second radio.

"Abe, are you there? We have a real emergency. Can you come?" I picked up my mike.

"Yes, Susie, hold everything! I'm on my way and should be home in 45 minutes."

When I landed back home I heard the story. A wicked man had attacked his two wives with a machete. I quickly refilled my gas tank and, with my stretcher on board, I took off. In 20 minutes I was over the last river and, as I circled for a landing, I saw the people waving. They were glad to see me come. The landing strip looked good and was clear of animals, so I landed. Many of the town's people came running down the hill to meet me, thanking me for coming and carrying the stretcher for me.

As we walked into the village, we saw the man who had done this terrible deed. He was all tied up against a post in the palaver hut (where people brought their problems to the chief). If even just one woman died, he would have to hang on that same rope with which he was tied.

The younger woman had received just one slash on her head before she managed to run away, but he had cornered the older one and just kept hacking away until the people were able to subdue him. By that time she had suffered five major cuts. I just don't understand why she didn't bleed to death. We carried her on my stretcher and rolled her, feet first, into the baggage compartment, while the other wife sat beside her.

I flew the the women straight to the city of Buchanan, where our son Darrell was church-planting. When I buzzed over his house, he jumped on his Honda motorbike and raced to the airfield to meet me. "Darrell, this is an emergency. Please go quickly and call the ambulance." He wheeled around immediately. Soon the women were being well cared for in the hospital. The husband stayed in jail until the women were healed, and then he was released. After all, they were his property.

Forced Landing into Gray Town

From morning on, I had been flying, helping so many people and dodging so many storms that I was really drained. Two young interns and a nurse were with me now, going to Ganta. They seemed so nervous about the terrible weather that I landed at the cocoa plantation, thinking they could catch a ride from there. But none was available. "If you are not too scared, I will take you on to Ganta," I offered.

"OK," they said, so up we went again into the clouds and rain. In ten minutes we arrived. I had two more flights left before dark, one of which was to carry the last of the members of the mission field's executive committee from Yila to Tappi. Ray Dunn and I landed in the rain at Yila. We hollered for John Vanden Akker to come quickly; then off we flew again into the rain. Though the sun had not yet set, it was quite dark because of the black clouds.

As we flew on, with rain pelting my windshield and the clouds covering all the hills, navigation became extremely difficult. To be sure I wouldn't miss Tappi, I angled a little to the left. I wanted to make sure I reached the only road and did not fly past it to be lost in the darkness. By the time we were over the road, the sky was so dark that a car coming along the road had its lights on. But where was Tappi? Oh no—it was completely blotted out in that black cloud and heavy rain. Underneath us lay the small village of Gray, so I shouted to John and Ray over the engine noise, "We are going to land on the road in the middle of that small town, so pray!" I didn't want to be lost in the darkness.

I swung around, lined up with the road and, approaching as low as I dared, I slipped in over the last trees, clipping off one branch. When my tires hit the road, I slammed on the brakes with all my strength. The plane skidded to a sudden stop. We stopped so quickly that all of us were surprised. I think the Lord put His hand on the tail to slow us down. The people, too, were surprised and happy, knowing we had escaped death, and they praised the Lord with us. One woman brought us three beautiful bananas and said, "We thank God too much!"

Then the car that we had seen from the air arrived and gave us a ride to the mission. Our meeting that night turned into a time of praise. The next morning the missionaries took me back to Gray to fly the plane out to the mission. With an empty plane now and full power, it was easy to pull up over the trees, and in a few minutes I was circling the mission to land. When I rolled to a stop, a dozen Christian women came from the dispensary, all with palm branches in their hands, circling around the plane and singing praises to the

Lord. It was a thrill to stand there with them, thanking and praising our great God!

Decorations and Farewells

On July 3, 1979, we, together with Ellie Munter, were called before a large gathering of the True Wig Party members of the Liberian government to be decorated for our many years of service to Liberia. One of our own Zondo boys, Joseph Gbadyu, had become an important man. The president had chosen him to be superintendent of Bassa County and appointed him to perform the ceremony to honor us.

Before all the dignitaries, he made an impressive speech, praising us for the work we had done. Then our good friend, the senior senator, Joshua Harmon, came and hung around each of our necks a beautiful gold star with the Liberian seal and logo on it and these words: "The love of liberty brought us here." The certificate of declaration read

I, William R. Tolbert, president of Liberia . . . ordain, constitute and appoint you KNIGHT COMMANDER OF THE LIBERIAN HUMANE ORDER OF THE STAR OF AFRICA.

It was signed by the president of Liberia.

In April 1980, after 35 years of service to Liberia, the time had come for us to leave. Dr. Allan E. Lewis, president of Baptist Mid-Missions, had written, asking me to come on staff as a deputation secretary for eleven northwestern states and half of Canada.

As we prepared to leave Liberia, our son Darrell advised us to book a flight out one week earlier to escape the possible uprising he sensed was brewing among the youth of Liberia. We took his advice and flew out on a Friday evening flight. Just five hours later, President Tolbert was shot in a coup led by Sergeant Samuel Doe, who then became the new president. All the previous presidents had been descendants of civilized American Negroes, but with Doe, a native, as president, there began to be much tribal jealousy, which spawned the recent bloody civil war. We are thankful that God protected Darrell and his family, as well as the other missionaries, during that first brief upheaval. Later, missionaries were advised to leave the country, and only a few non-Liberians were killed. But many of our Liberian people suffered horribly. Pray for them.

Epilogue

When we returned from Liberia in 1980, the Lord provided us with a new car and a new house that a friend had built. "Abe," he said, "it seems like the Lord told me to let you have this house that I'm building." Susie and I paid for his expenses up to that point; then we did a lot of the finishing ourselves with help from our family. We loved the house, and it has been just what we need.

Shortly after arriving home, I met with the council of Baptist Mid-Missions. During that first council meeting, the men asked me to say a few words. I told them, "I appreciate very much the privilege and challenge of this new ministry and your confidence in me. But the immensity of the task reminds me of the man who was condemned to 99 years in jail.

"He wailed, 'But judge, how am I going to do all that?'

"The judge replied, 'You try to do as much as you can.' "

Then I said, "I will try to do as much as I can, but don't you think you should buy me a small Lear jet to cover this large territory?" They all chuckled, but I never did get one!

The way our churches welcomed us into our new ministry of recruitment was a blessing to see. Traveling, of course, includes many dangers on the road and in the air. Susie always goes with me in the motorhome but not when I fly. We have been twice around the United States and Canada, twice to Alaska, once to Mexico, fifteen times across the United States. I have also made about thirty flights on commercial airlines to the East, always in a recruiting ministry.

On one of my flights coming into Winnipeg, the landing gear on the Air Canada flight did not seem to lock properly. We flew around and around till our fuel was about gone; then we came in and landed safely. Some of the passengers were really scared though.

On an all-night flight to Toronto, I had planned to sleep some, but when the nice young lady beside me became interested in my testimony and the Bible I shared with her, I could not sleep. After a while I asked her if she, too, would like to be saved, and she said, "Yes!" I led her to the Lord somewhere over Montana at about 40,000 feet of altitude at 2:00 A.M. Then she began to bubble, and I rejoiced with her. We could not sleep as we excitedly shared the things of God and eternity during the rest of the trip.

Susie and I were rolling along in our motorhome on the freeway in Washington, D.C., when car horns began to blare all around us. I looked in the mirror and saw a great cloud of smoke billowing from behind our rig. Just ahead of us was an off ramp, so I coasted onto the island. An oil line had burst, and the oil was pouring onto the hot manifold. Fortunately there was no fire. Praise God! Soon a highway "Trouble Truck" pulled up ahead of us and gave me some more oil. I was able to fix the break, so we were on our way again. How good the Lord has been!

On the last Alaska trip, we had a flat tire. There was no place to fix it for a hundred miles in each direction, but just a stone's throw away, there *was*. Isn't that wonderful? Great is our God!

In Liberia I always had to dodge birds and, in the later years, airplanes. I remember coming through the Roberts Field Airport control zone. The tower cleared me through and then radioed, "A Pan Am Clipper is coming in. Can you see him?"

"Yes, I can," I replied.

"Why don't you talk to him," the controller suggested. That was unusual, so I called him.

"Hello Big Brother. I hope the slip stream from my Piper Cub won't upset your landing too much!" He came back with a chuckle.

"Thanks, Little Brother. I will be careful!"

Here at home, I don't have to dodge birds or airplanes, but one day we had to dodge a flying outhouse!! Driving through the state of Washington, we were following a truck that had two outhouses on the back of it. Susie commented, "They sure don't look very stable to me, the way they are teetering around." I agreed. In the next instant, while I glanced in my mirror to see a big truck bearing down on us from the rear, Susie shouted, "Here it comes!" Sure enough, one outhouse came flying down right in front of us. The Lord made it kind of spin on its side toward the middle of the road, however, so I was able to slip by to let the truck behind me take care of it. (He made it past as well.)

It has been such a blessing to see the hand of the Lord still on us, planning and guiding all our ways. It also has been a blessing to see the way the Lord has used our children. Darrell and Donna Guenter, with their two sons, ministered first in Liberia and then in New Zealand as missionaries for 13 years and now as pastor in Northfield, Massachusetts. We have rejoiced to see the way Suzanne and her husband, Wayne Bertness, have grown in their ministry. He is a ventriloquist, and they have trained their four children to sing and help in their children's evangelism work in churches all over North

America. They travel in a big bus, which is their home and their school for the children too.

Wesley, our ship-captain son, and Brenda, his school-teacher wife, have made us proud too. They built a 45-foot catamaran boat at Mahone Bay, Nova Scotia. They plan to go sailing for one year. Perhaps they will even go to Liberia. In October 1991, they sailed down the coast to North Carolina, where they are finishing the boat during the winter months. They won't come back to Halifax, Nova Scotia, until October 1992. We plan to see them in September in the Boston area.

Grandchildren are the nicest people, and we have eight of them. Darrell has two boys, and Suzanne has three girls and a boy. Wesley has a boy and a girl, Jim and Dawn. They, as well as their mother, Margaret Guenter, live near Grand Rapids, Michigan. We drop in there to see them every chance we get.

Now that we are officially retired, it feels good to coast a bit. But we still have an ongoing ministry in many ways. We still travel and preach for the Lord. Our little motorhome, decorated with Bible texts on all sides, is a joy for cruising through traffic. We get varied reactions.

In California we pulled up to a red light, and a guy pulled up alongside us. He hollered, "Yes, I want some! Give me some; I need it!" I quickly passed him some tracts, and he hollered back, "That's it; I need to be saved." The lights changed, and we lost him; but we trust the Lord found him.

Three Christian men pulled up to us where we were stopped on the highway. They were so excited to see the witness of our motorhome on the road that one man gave me a $50 bill to help us along the way. God says His Word will not return to Him void, so we keep planting.

We want to thank all our friends and churches that have stood with us in prayers and in a material way through the many years. Without them all, our ministry would have been impossible. God bless you richly!

One day God will reward each one for his faithfulness according to his works. What a day that will be! Praise God! "For this God is our God for ever and ever: he will be our guide even unto death" (Ps. 48:14).